Studying for a
DRIVER'S LICENSE

Dr. Frank C. Kenel

and

Beverly Vaillancourt

The Peoples Publishing Group, Inc.

Free to Learn, to Grow, to Change

Credits

Writers: Dr. Frank C. Kenel and Beverly Vaillancourt
Editing by Jocelyn Chu
Copyediting by Salvatore Allocco
Photo and Editorial Assistance by Daniel Ortiz, Jr.
Design by Dr. Frank C. Kenel and Beverly Vaillancourt
Photo Research by Dr. Frank C. Kenel and Beverly Vaillancourt
Spanish Translation by Nora Adams, Director of the Learning Center,
    Felician College
Cover Design by Klaus G. Spitzenberger, Westchester Graphics Group, Inc.
Logo Design by Wendy Kury
Electronic Publishing Consultant: James Fee Langendoen
Reader Reviews by Jerome Gooch, Dorothy Gammon, Past President,
    Illinois Driver's Education, and Percy H. Benedict, President of the
    American Driver and Traffic Safety Education Association

Permissions and Photo Credits:
All photographic material provided courtesy of the American Automobile
Association, Traffic Safety and Engineering Department, Heathrow, Florida.
A special thanks to Dr. Charles Butler, Director of Driver's Education
Programs, and Marquita Dudley, Driver Safety Coordinator. Many thanks to
the driver's education teachers around the country who participated in a
research survey relating to this book.

Printed in the United States of America.

9 8

Table of Contents

Before You Begin

We would like to share a few moments with you.

This book will help you to learn about the traffic laws, signs, signals, and road markings you must know to get a driver"s license. These traffic laws, signs, signals, and road markings help to guide your actions when you drive. This book also will help you to learn what you must do to get a license for a car.

Written in a clear, simple way, this book can help you to become a safer driver. It explains what traffic laws say and what drivers should do. This book shows and explains types of traffic signs, signals, and road markings.

Just knowing the laws and other things explained in this book will not keep you out of a crash. Yet, knowing traffic laws, and what they mean, can help you to predict what other road users may do. Obeying traffic laws also help other drivers to predict what you may do.

New drivers often make mistakes. Sometimes they do not see things as they really are. At times, they are not aware of what to look for, or do not know what to expect of other drivers. New drivers are in many more crashes than drivers who have been driving a few years. It seems to take about five years before a new driver learns to drive as well as the average driver.

There are traffic laws that many drivers do not seem to understand. Sometimes drivers simply choose not to obey the law. Not obeying laws concerning the use of alcohol, other drugs and driving, right-of-way, speed limits, passing, and other use of headlights can lead to serious accidents.

The laws in this book are based on the *Uniform Vehicle Code* (UVC). The traffic signs, signals, and markings in this book are based on the *Manual On Uniform Traffic Control Devices* (MUTCD).

Not all traffic laws in every state are the same as the UVC. Your state, or some cities in your state, may use signs or signals no shown in the MUTCD. When this happens, information in a yellow bar and black letters will direct you to check your state driver's manual. Look for this yellow box.

Watch for all information boxed in a green bar and dropout. This is information you must know to pass your driver's test. Also watch for information boxed in a red and dropout or marked by a thunderbolt. These are safety facts you must know. Information boxed in a blue color bar and dropout tells about things we thought you would like to know.

We wish you well in your effort to get your driver's license. We hope you have many years of crash free driving. Remember–a good driver is someone with whom you feel safe and like to ride.

Sincere best wishes,

Dr. Francis C. Kenel
Beverly Vaillancourt, M.Ed.

SECTION 1: TRAFFIC LAWS and YOU

CHAPTER 1: What You Need to Know about Driving

Before you read, you should know that:

▶ a **traffic law** is a rule that tells you what to do, or not to do, when driving;

▶ **legal** means to agree with the law;

▶ a **vehicle** (VEE-hih-kl) is any car, truck, bus, bicycle, or anything else with wheels that can by law use a road for travel;

▶ a **crash** is one vehicle hitting another vehicle or object;

▶ **risk** means to take a chance.

After reading this chapter, you should be able to:

▶ give two reasons why we have traffic laws;

▶ tell what age group is most likely to get into a crash;

▶ tell how driving in a **legal** way can help you stay out of a crash.

CHECK YOUR STATE MANUAL The traffic laws talked about in this book are from a special book called the *Uniform Vehicle Code (UVC)*. Sometimes traffic laws in a state are not all the same as the UVC laws.

When this happens, you will be asked to check your state driving book. This book is called the *State Driver's Manual* (MAN-yoo-al). You must know the traffic rules for your state to pass your driver's test.

The purpose of this book is to make you a safe driver. To do this, you will need to learn about traffic laws. Using traffic laws will help you to drive in a safe way.

Knowing traffic laws will help you to pass your driver's test. You need to pass a driver's test before you can drive a vehicle on your own. Knowing traffic laws also will help you predict, or tell before it happens, what other road users might do.

Every driver must be a responsible (ree-SPON-sih-bl) driver. A responsible driver tries to drive safely. Responsible drivers always watch for mistakes other drivers might make. Responsible drivers try to obey traffic laws. They let other drivers go first. They drive smoothly. People who ride with responsible drivers feel safe and at ease.

▲ Knowing traffic laws will help you to pass your driver's test.

▼ Drivers who are 16 to 25 years old get into more crashes than drivers of any other age.

WATCH OUT !

Drivers who are 16 to 25 years old get into more **crashes** than drivers of other ages. Drivers of this age group also are more likely to die in a crash.

Crashes usually happen because a traffic law has been broken. Perhaps the driver did not stop when the law said the driver should stop. Perhaps the driver was driving too closely to another vehicle. Maybe the driver was driving on the wrong part of the road. When there is a crash, most of the time it is the young driver who has broken a traffic law.

Many traffic laws grew from customs or ways people traveled in the past. These customs made travel easier. As people used new ways for traveling, customs that worked became laws.

People in the United States drive on the right side of the road. Why? Well, it may surprise you to know . . . .

Before people used cars and trucks for traveling, they used covered wagons. Horses or oxen pulled the wagons. The driver sat on a wooden seat that was high off the ground. The reins (ranz) for the horses were held in the driver's left hand. The reins guided the horses. The driver's right hand held a long whip. The driver used the whip to make the horses start or go faster.

Under the driver's right foot was a wooden lever. The lever worked the wagon's brakes. Because of all this, it was easier for wagon drivers to drive on the right side of the road. But just like the wagon drivers of the past, we drive on the right side of the road!

▲ Conestoga or covered wagon drivers of the past also drove on the right side of the road.

Traffic laws are laws that tell how you must drive on the road. They tell you what you can and cannot do. Traffic laws help you predict what the driver of some other vehicle should do.

They also tell you what other road users should do. Other road users could be people riding bikes, motorcycles, or just walking.

Drivers who do not follow traffic rules **risk** getting into a crash. A crash could mean damage to your car, being hurt, or being killed. Anyone in the car you hit also could be hurt or be killed.

Knowing traffic laws helps you to drive in a legal way. Driving in a legal way helps to reduce (ree-DUS), or make smaller, your risk of getting into a crash. Driving in a legal way will reduce the chance that you will make a mistake when you are driving.

It can help you see problems better while driving. Driving in a legal way will help to give you time to think about how you must drive. It also will help you predict what other drivers might do.

Drive Smart!

Directions: Read each sentence. Draw a line under that the word that makes the sentence correct. Then write why the sentence is true.

1. Drivers who do not follow traffic laws are (more, less) likely to be in a crash.

   _____

   _____

2. Driving in a legal way will (always, usually) keep you out of a crash.

   _____

   _____

3. Driving in a legal way helps you to (predict, risk) what another driver should do.

   _____

   _____

The People's Publishing Group, Inc.:*Studying for a Driver's License*

Hints to Help You Pass that Test!

Multiple Choice Tests

Here are some ways to do well on multiple choice tests. You will find multiple choice questions on the written part of your driver's license test.

Hint # 1

Read each choice carefully. One small word can change the whole meaning of your choice.

New drivers
a. often get in car crashes.
b. get in car crashes more often.

Hint # 2

Carefully read the statement that comes before the choices. Check the choice you made with the beginning statement.

Once you get a license to drive, you may drive
a. only at night.
b. any size of vehicle.
c. only the size of vehicle for which you applied.

Hint # 3

Look for words such as, "always", "never", "all", and "none". Before you choose an answer with any of these words in it, make sure they correctly apply or match the meaning.

Which people are most often in crashes?
a. all people ages 16-24 years
b. people age 16-24 years
c. always people under 30 years of age

Hint # 4

Guess! You should be able to rule out or say NO to at least two of the four choices, just because of what you know. If you are unsure which of the other two answers are correct, make your best guess. You may be right.

Remember! This is a driving test. Something you do not know may get you in a crash. After taking the test, look back in this book for the correct answer. This short moment of your time may save your life. Remember: Driving smart means driving safe!

Hint # 5

Do not give up! First, work on the questions that have answers you quickly know. Then go back to the questions that have answers which gave you some trouble. Read them again carefully. Think things through. If you are still not sure, try Hint #4.

Hint # 6

Change answers if you really feel you may have made the wrong choice. Yes, remember:

* First finish the whole test
* Then carefully reread questions you have a hunch or idea might be answered incorrectly
* Change any wrong choices
* Make sure you erase your first answer.

Section 1 Review   TRAFFIC LAWS AND YOU

Directions: These questions come from Chapter 1. You may look back to this chapter if you need help in choosing the correct answer. Remember to read each sentence carefully. Then write X beside the answer you choose.

CHAPTER 1 What You Need to Know Before You Drive

1. Obeying traffic laws
   ___ a.   means you have to drive slowly.
   ___ b.   means it will take more time to get where you want to go.
   ___ c.   helps other road users better predict what you are going to do.
   ___ d.   gives you the right-of-way.

2. The group of drivers most often in crashes are
   ___ a.   over 65 years of age.
   ___ b.   45 to 64 years of age.
   ___ c.   25 to 44 years of age.
   ___ d.   16 to 24 years of age.

3. Most people who have crashes have not broken a traffic law.
   ___ True
   ___ False

4. Most drivers who are in crashes know about traffic laws.
   ___ True
   ___ False

5. Responsible drivers try to see dangers ahead.
   ___ True
   ___ False

SECTION 2: LICENSING
CHAPTER 2: Your License to Drive

Before you read, you should know that:

▶ a **permit** is a card that lets a person drive for a short time while the person prepares to take the driver's test;

▶ a **license** is a card that shows that a person has passed all state tests needed to drive;

▶ a **highway** is a road used by vehicles. Other words used for highway are road, street, and roadway.

After reading this chapter, you should be able to:

▶ list what is needed to get a **permit**;

▶ list what is needed to get a **license**.

PASS THAT TEST !

Getting a License

Everyone must have a license to drive on a **highway.** You get one kind of license for driving a car. You must have a different kind of license to drive large trucks, buses, and other vehicles.

A driver's license gives a person the right to drive on the streets of the state. A driver's license is issued (IH-shood), or given, for a number of years. The license can be taken away by the state if a driver gets too many traffic tickets. It also can be taken away if a driver has a number of crashes.

You must have your driver's license with you anytime you drive. You must show your driver's license to any police officer who asks to see it.

You must fill out a form to get a driver's license. On the form, you must write in these things:
- your name, address and sex (male or female);
- proof of when you were born;
- your age;
- if you have ever had a license before.

You must pass a test before you get your driver's license. On your test, you will need to:
- prove you see well without glasses (or with glasses if you must wear them).
- show that you can read and that you know about traffic laws.
- know all road signs and road markings.
- show you can drive a car the right way.

CHECK YOUR STATE MANUAL
Getting a Permit
A permit is given to someone who is learning to drive. Depending on state law, a permit lets a driver drive for six, nine or twelve months. Traffic laws for most states say that a person with a driver's license must be with the person driving with a permit.

▼ You must have your driver's license with you anytime you drive.

CHECK YOUR STATE MANUAL

The age when you may first get a license is not the same in every state. In most states, a person must be 16 to get a driver's license. Sometimes, a 15-year-old may get a license.

In some states a 16-year-old may not drive between midnight and 5 A.M. In other states, a 16-year-old may only drive if a parent or other adult is present in the car. The 16-year-old may have to do this for a few months.

WATCH OUT !

If you are under 18, the form you fill out to get a license must be signed by your father, mother, or other adult who watches over you. The adult who signs your form may write to the state to ask that your license be taken away.

Drive Smart!

Directions: Read each sentence. If the sentence is true or correct, put an X in the TRUE box. If the sentence is not true, put an X in the FALSE box. Rewrite each false sentence to make it true.

1. Passing the test to drive a car means that by law, you also can drive a bus or large truck.

   TRUE ☐   FALSE ☒

   _____

   _____

2. You must pass a test that tells how well you see before you can get a driver's license.

   TRUE ☐   FALSE ☐

   _____

   _____

3. It is not legal for a 16-year-old to drive between the hours of midnight and 5 A.M. in your state.

   TRUE ☐   FALSE ☐

   _____

   _____

4. If you are under 18 years of age, the person who signed your driver's license form may write to the state and ask that the license be taken away.

    TRUE ☐   FALSE ☑

    _____

    _____

5. You do not have to know about every road sign used in your state to get a driver's license.

    TRUE ☐   FALSE ☐

    _____

    _____

STUDENT NOTES

```



```

CHAPTER 3: A License for Your Vehicle

▲ You need to register to get license plates for a vehicle so you can drive the vehicle on a road.

CHECK YOUR STATE MANUAL In both Maine and Alabama, the title law is only for vehicles beginning with model year 1975. In some states, the title law is only for vehicles that are less than 10 years old.

CHECK YOUR STATE MANUAL Some states say a car must have two license plates. One plate is put on the front of the car. One license is put on the back of the car.

Some states say that every car on the road must have insurance. In these states, you must prove that you have insurance before you can get new license plates or tags.

The **insurance** some states say you must have will pay for any injury or damage you may cause to other people. States often say how much insurance you must have. States do not say you must have insurance to cover any damage or injury to you, your vehicle or property (PROP-er-tee).

Before you read, you should know that:

▶ a title is a paper given by the state that shows who owns a vehicle;

▶ ID is short for identification (eye-den-tih-fih-KA-shun); anything that names a person, or thing;

▶ a lien is a statement of ownership of a vehicle by the person or business you are borrowing money from to buy a vehicle;

▶ to register means to get license plates for a vehicle so you can drive the vehicle on a road;

▶ insurance is a written contract that keeps you from having to pay a large amount of money in case of a crash.

After reading this chapter, you should be able to:

▶ list the things needed to get a title;

▶ list the things needed to get a license for your car.

PASS THAT TEST !

Getting a Title

Every vehicle owner must send in a form to get a title. The title shows who owns the vehicle. When you fill out the form to get a title, you must tell these things:

- your name and address;

- the kind of car you have;

- the special number given to the car, called the car's Vehicle **ID** Number (VIN);

- the number of cylinders (SIL-in-derz) the car has;

- the number of miles the car has been driven so far;

- if the new car is new or used;

- the date you bought the car;

- the name of the person or group who sold you the car;

- if someone holds a **lien** or claim on the car.

Getting a License for Your Car

You must **register** your car. To do this, you will fill out a form. On the form you must say:

- your name and address;

- the kind of car;

- the insurance company you use (in states that say you must have insurance on a vehicle before you can drive it).

After you register your car, you will get a registration (rej-is-TRA-shun) card. The registration card must be kept on the vehicle. You must show the registration card to any police officer who asks to see it.

Along with your registration card, you will get a license plate. You will not get a new plate every year. Instead, most years, you will get a sticker to put on the license plate. The sticker is called a tag. You will be told where to put the tag.

If you are under 18 years of age, the form you fill out to register your car must be signed by your father, mother or person who cares for you. The person who signs your form to register your car may also ask the state in writing to take it away.

Crash Basics

What to do if in a crash:

- Stop as close to the place of the crash as possible.

- Try to stop in a place where you will not be a danger to other vehicles.

- Call the police.

- Stay by the crash area.

- Show your driver's license or permit to the police or to anyone who is part of the crash.

- Tell who owns the vehicle.

- Show the vehicle registration card.

▲ Make sure you know what to do if you are in a crash. Learn the crash basics!

DID YOU KNOW?

Since 1901, New York state car owners have had to register their cars. In 1907, Connecticut passed the first state driver license law. The last state to adopt a driver license law was South Dakota in 1955.

Drive Smart!

Directions: Fill in the blank with the correct word or words.

1. In the state in which you live, you _____ have insurance to register a vehicle.

2. If you only get one license plate, it goes on the _____ of your vehicle.

3. A vehicle registration form for anyone under 18 years old must be signed by _____.

4. If you buy a vehicle with money you have borrowed from a bank, the bank will be shown as having a _____ on the title of the vehicle.

5. After you register your vehicle, you will get a registration _____ and one or two _____.

STUDENT NOTES

Hints to Help You Pass that Test!

True - False Tests

True - False questions often deal with facts. Many True - False questions are written to trap students who do not know all their facts. To do well on True - False questions, follow these hints.

Hint # 1

Read carefully. Read every word. The whole sentence needs to be either all true or all false.

True or False
To get a driver's license you must pass a written test from every state.

Hint # 2

Look for words that change the meaning of the sentence. Such words are, "all", "only", "always", "because", and "none".

True or False
All states allow drivers under 18 to drive between midnight and 4 A.M.

True or False
Only people who have driven before may get a new license when they move to a new state.

Hint # 3

Guess! You have a 50/50 chance of being right. Again, remember to check any answer you were unsure of after taking the test.

Hint # 4

Do not change your answers. In True - False tests, your first hunch is most often correct.

True or False
Knowing traffic laws, signs, signals, and pavement markings will help you to be a responsible driver.

True or False
Registering your car means you have paid for your car.

Section 2 Review   LICENSING

Directions: These questions come from Chapters 2 and 3. You may look back to these chapters if you need help in choosing the correct answer. Remember to read each sentence carefully. Then write X beside the answer you choose.

CHAPTER 2 Your License to Drive

1. To get a drivers license you must
   ___ a.   be at least 18 years old.
   ___ b.   agree not to drive after dark.
   ___ c.   pass a written test, have your vision checked, and show that you are able to drive in a safe way.
   ___ d.   agree to drive only with your parents in the car for at least six (6) months.

2. In the state in which you live, to apply for a driver's license before you are 18 years old, you must
   ___ a.   pass driver education and have a birth certificate.
   ___ b.   pass driver education, have a birth certificate, and your parents must sign for you.
   ___ c.   have a birth certificate and your parents must sign for you.
   ___ d.   have had a learner's permit for at least six (6) months.

3. Before a person under 18 years of age can get a driver's license they must apply for a learner's permit.
   ___ True
   ___ False

4. Some states do not allow drivers under 18 years to drive between midnight and 5 A.M.
   ___ True
   ___ False

CHAPTER 3 A License for Your Car

1. In the state in which you live, when you register a car, you
   ___ a.   must have car insurance and your parents must sign for you if you are not 18.
   ___ b.   do not need car insurance, but your parents must sign for you if you are not 18.

2. In the state in which you live, when you register a car, you receive a registration card and
   ___ a.   one license plate that goes on the front of your car.
   ___ b.   one license plate that goes on the back of your car.
   ___ c.   two license plates, one for the front and one for the back of your car.

3. You cannot register a car if you do not have a title for it.
   ___ True
   ___ False

4. If you are in a traffic crash, you must stop as close as possible to the crash, tell who you are, get help, and call the police if needed.
   ___ True
   ___ False

The People's Publishing Group, Inc.:*Studying for a Driver's License*

SECTION 3: MOVING in TRAFFIC

All drivers must drive by the laws that say how traffic must move. A driver must follow what a police officer, firefighter, flagperson, or crossing guard says to do.

CHAPTER 4: Driving on the Right Side of the Road

Before you read, you should know that:

▶ **driving to the right** means to drive to the right side of the center of the road.

▶ a **lane** is an area divided by white or yellow lines;

▶ a **traffic island** (EYE-land) is a solid area that divides traffic.

▶ a **traffic circle** is an area where all traffic flows in the same way or direction (dy-REK-shun) around a circle.

After reading this chapter, you should be able to:

▶ tell what it means to **drive on the right side;**

▶ list the times when you can drive on the left side.

▲ Driving to the right means to drive to the right side of the center of the road.

PASS THAT TEST !

All drivers must drive on the right side of the road.

Drivers of slow vehicles must drive as far to the right as they can.

There are times when you may drive left of the center of the road. You may do so when:

• you are passing another vehicle;

• you must drive around something that is blocking the road;

• you are driving on a three-lane road;

• you are using a shared left-turn **lane**.

When driving on a one-way street, you may drive only the way shown on the sign.

You must drive to the right side of the **traffic island** when you drive into a **traffic circle.**

▼ No driver may drive left of center on roads with two or more lanes of traffic moving the same way.

WATCH OUT !

No driver may drive left of center on roads with two or more lanes of traffic moving the same way.

Drive Smart!

Directions: Read the sentence part. Then put a check in each box next to the words that finish the sentence in a correct way.

You may drive left of center when

☐ you are passing.

☐ you are going around another vehicle.

☐ there are three lanes of traffic moving in the same way.

☐ you are using a shared left-turn lane.

☐ you are driving next to a traffic island.

Directions: Label each of these pictures. Draw an arrow on each picture showing the direction in which you should drive.

▲ One-way street

▲ Traffic island

▲ Traffic circle

CHAPTER 5: Passing

Before you read, you should know that:

- to **pass** means to catch up to and get ahead, or in front of, another vehicle;

- to **signal** means to tell other road users where you are or what you want to do;

- to **steer** means to guide a vehicle by holding the steering wheel and turning it right or left;

- an **intersection** (in-ter-SEK-shun) is where one road crosses or joins another road;

- **MPH** means **miles per hour,** the number of miles traveled in one hour.

After reading this chapter, you will be able to:

- tell how to **pass** to the left;

- list when you may pass to the right.

PASS THAT TEST !

Passing to the Left
You must pass to the left on a two-lane road. To pass you must:

- check vehicles traveling ahead of you;

- check ahead for driveways, crossroads, pedestrians, and other roadway users;

- look to see if there are any vehicles coming toward you;

- check how close you are to oncoming vehicles (vehicles coming toward you);

- check your mirrors to see if anyone behind you is trying to pass;

- **signal** that you are going to pass;

- check over your left shoulder to see if someone is passing you;

- make sure you have lots of time to pass the slow vehicle;

- pass the slow vehicle;

- signal that you plan to return to your lane;

- **steer** back into your lane when you can see the front end of the vehicle you have passed in your rear view mirror;

- make sure there are at least 200 feet between you and the oncoming vehicle when you steer back to your lane.

▲ You must pass to the left on a two-lane road.

▲ You may pass to the right of the vehicle ahead of you when there are two or more lanes of traffic moving in the same direction.

WATCH OUT !

Passing on a two-lane road is very risky. It is against the law to go over the speed limit to pass another vehicle. There are more than 5,000 people killed each year in head-on crashes.

You may not pass to the left when:

- driving near the top of a hill;

- driving toward a curve;

- within 100 feet of any kind of **intersection,** bridge, or railroad crossing.

- signs and markings say passing is not allowed.

WATCH OUT !

You should stay to the right of your lane when you are being passed. Keep a steady speed. Be ready to slow down, if necessary.

DID YOU KNOW?

It takes only 13 seconds to pass another vehicle. They are right if you are going 40 **mph** and the vehicle you want to pass is going 30 mph. If you are going 60 mph and the vehicle you want to pass is going 50 mph, it will take 19 seconds. If the vehicle is an 18-wheel semi (seh-MEE) truck, it will take about 23 seconds to pass.

At 40 mph, you are moving about 60 feet per second. A vehicle going 30 mph is moving about 45 feet per second. You are moving about 15 feet per second faster than the vehicle you want to pass. You should start to pass about 2 seconds (120 feet) behind the vehicle. Then steer back into your lane 1 second (60 feet) ahead of the vehicle.

Remember that at 40 mph you will travel about 780 feet in 13 seconds. But an oncoming vehicle is also traveling 780 feet in 13 seconds. You need about one-third of a mile to pass a vehicle. At one-third of a mile, an oncoming vehicle looks like it is not moving.

PASS THAT TEST !

Passing to the Right

You may pass to the right of the vehicle ahead of you when:

- there are two or more lanes of traffic moving the same way;

- the vehicle ahead of you is turning left.

You should stay to the right of your lane when you are being passed. Keep a steady speed. Be ready to slow down, if necessary.

WATCH OUT !

You should not pass a school bus that is stopped when you are on a two-lane road. However, you may pass the bus if you are on the other side of a divided highway. You also may pass a school bus if you are told to do so by a police officer or school bus driver.

Do not pass a vehicle if it has stopped at a crosswalk to let a person cross the road.

Drive Smart!

Directions: Read each sentence. If the sentence is true, or correct, put an X in the TRUE box. If the sentence is not true, put an X in the FALSE box. Rewrite each false sentence to make it true.

1. You must always give a signal when you want to pass.

   TRUE ☐   FALSE ☐

   _____

   _____

   _____

   _____

2. You may not pass to the right of a car that is stopped and waiting to make a left turn on a two-lane road.

   TRUE ☐   FALSE ☐

   _____

   _____

   _____

   _____

3. It is against the law to speed up when passing another car.

   TRUE ☐   FALSE ☐

   _____

   _____

   _____

   _____

4. List four places where it is not legal to pass on the left on a two-lane road.

   1. _____

   _____

   2. _____

   _____

   3. _____

   _____

   4. _____

   _____

5. List the two times it is OK to pass a school bus that is stopped with its red lights flashing.

   1. _____

   _____

   2. _____

   _____

STUDENT NOTES

CHAPTER 6: Right-of-Way

Before you read, you should know that:

- **right-of-way** means that one driver is given the right to move before another driver moves;

- a **traffic sign** is a sign that tells drivers things they need to know;

- a **traffic signal** is a sign or light that warns or directs drivers to take some action;

- an **emergency** (ee-MER-jen-see) **vehicle** is a vehicle with flashing lights and a siren used to respond to calls for help;

- a **pedestrian** (peh-DES-tree-en) is any person walking along or across a roadway;

After reading this chapter, you should be able to:

- list six situations (sit-yoo-AY-shuns) or places where a driver should give someone else the **right-of-way;**

- tell how right-of-way is used in each listed situation.

⚡ Right-of-way is something a driver gives to another roadway user. In many cases, right-of-way is controlled by a **traffic sign** or a **traffic signal.**

▼ Right-of-way is something a driver gives to another roadway user.

PASS THAT TEST !

Here are eleven places where right-of-way is given. You must know these situations.

1. At a corner that does not have traffic signs or signals:

   The driver on the left shall give right-of-way to the driver on the right.

2. At a four-way stop:

   The first car to stop shall be given the right-of-way.

3. Police cars, fire engines and ambulances (AM-byoo-lan-sez) have the right of way.

   On a two-lane road, when an **emergency** vehicle is using its flashing lights and siren, other drivers must steer to the right side of the road and stop. The drivers must stay stopped until the emergency vehicle has passed.

   You do not need to stop if the emergency vehicle is on the other side of a divided highway.

4. Drivers going straight (strayt) are to be given the right-of-way by drivers turning left. Turning left means to steer the vehicle to the left.

▼ When an emergency vehicle is using its flashing lights and the siren is sounded, other drivers must steer to the right side of the road and stop.

▲ Any vehicle entering a road from the side road must give the right-of-way.

5. Any vehicle entering or crossing a road from the side of the road, driveway or alley must give the right-of-way to all vehicles on the road.

6. Drivers wishing to drive into a traffic circle must give the right-of-way to the vehicles in the traffic circle.

7. Drivers wishing to enter an intersection must give the right-of-way to vehicles already in the intersection.

8. Drivers making a right turn after stopping at a stop sign or traffic signal must give the right-of-way to any crossing vehicle or person. A **right turn** means that the vehicle is steered to the right.

9. Drivers must give the right-of-way to road workers or machines (muh-SHEENZ).

10. Drivers must give the right-of-way to **pedestrians** in the crosswalk.

11. Drivers must give the right-of-way to any blind person who is using a white cane or seeing eye dog.

Drive Smart!

Directions: Picture each story in your mind. Think about it carefully. Then write how right-of-way is given in each situation.

1. **Situation:** You are coming to a traffic circle. There are a lot of cars in the traffic circle. Other cars are coming into the circle.
   Who should give the right-of-way? Explain why.

   _____

   _____

   _____

2. **Situation:** You are driving on a two lane road. Traffic is not heavy. You hear a siren and see a police car coming toward you with its lights flashing.
   Who should give the right-of-way? Explain why.

   _____

   _____

   _____

3. **Situation:** You want to turn right at the corner. There is a stop sign at the corner. As you stop for the stop sign, you see a pedestrian waiting to cross the road.
Who should give the right-of-way? Explain why.

_____

_____

_____

4. **Situation:** You have picked up a box at a store. Now you have to enter a street from an alley. Buildings on both sides of the alley make it hard to see pedestrians or vehicles.
Who should give the right-of-way? Explain why.

_____

_____

_____

5. **Situation:** You are going to a dance across town. First, you must stop to buy some gas for your car. You want to turn left across traffic into a gas station. Three vehicles are coming toward you.
Who should give the right-of-way? Explain why.

_____

_____

_____

CHAPTER 7: Turning and Lane Changes

Before you read, you should know that:

▶ a *turn* is a move to another street at a corner or into a driveway or parking space;

▶ a *signal lamp* is a brake light, turn signal, or emergency flasher.

After reading this chapter, you should be able to:

▶ tell what you must do before you **turn** or make a lane change;

▶ list the steps for making a right turn;

▶ list the steps for making a left turn;

▶ tell how to turn from a one-way street.

A driver must always signal before turning or making a lane change. A driver must always make sure a turn or lane change can be made safely before making a move.

▲ A driver must always signal before turning or making a lane change

PASS THAT TEST !

Signaling for a Turn or Lane Change

You must signal before making a turn. You must signal at least 100 feet before you turn.

The signal may be given by using a turn **signal lamp.**

The signal also may be given by using your left arm and hand.

PASS THAT TEST !

Changing Lanes

When you change lanes, you steer left or right from one lane to another. When you change lanes, you must give right of way to vehicles in those lanes. Before you change lanes, you must:

• check traffic ahead of you;

• check your outside mirror (MIR-or) for vehicles to the side of you;

• check your inside mirror for cars behind you;

• signal you want to change lanes;

• look over your right or left shoulder as needed for vehicles beside you;

• make the lane change only when it is safe.

Turning

You must do these things when you want to make a turn:

- place your vehicle in the proper lane;
- signal that you want to turn;
- check the traffic ahead of you;
- check the traffic coming toward you;
- use your mirrors to check traffic behind you;
- adjust the speed of your vehicle;
- check for traffic that crosses you (cross traffic);
- check for pedestrians;
- turn when it is safe to do so.

Turning Right

When you want to turn right, you must be in the right-hand lane of traffic. Sometimes, there is a special right-turn lane. Sometime there is a special turn lane is called a **bay.**

Most of the time, right-turn bays have a yield (yeeld) right-of-way sign. When you turn right, you must steer your turn into the first travel lane to the right.

You must do these things when you want to turn right:

- signal for a right turn;
- check the traffic coming toward you;
- check the traffic ahead of you;
- turn when it is safe;
- adjust the speed of your vehicle.

▲ A special right-turn lane is called a **bay.**

▼ You must be in the left lane to turn left. This car should be on the left.

Turning Left

You must be in the left lane to turn left. The left lane may be:

- next to the center line;
- next to the curb if it is a one-way street;
- a left-turn bay;
- If there is no cross traffic or pedestrians, you may move into the intersection.

▼ In a few states the law says you must signal 3 to 4 seconds ahead of a turn. Always signal early.

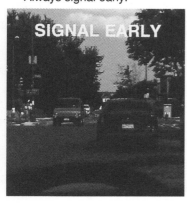

PASS THAT TEST !

Turn into the nearest left travel lane when turning left into a one-way street.

Turn into the first lane to the right of the center line or divider when turning into a two-way street.

You must do these things when you want to turn left:

- signal for a left turn;

- move into the intersection;

- stop if traffic is coming toward you;

- keep your wheels straight while you are stopped;

- keep your foot on the brake pedal until the oncoming vehicles have passed you;

- turn when it is safe to do so.

Turn into the nearest left travel lane if it is a one-way street. When turning into a two-way street, turn into the first lane to the right of the center line or divider.

PASS THAT TEST !

You must give the right-of-way to all other vehicles and pedestrians before turning.

Sometimes, there is more than one turn lane. When this happens, the lane you turn into must match the lane from which you began your turn.

PASS THAT TEST !

Turnabouts

Sometimes, you find you are going the wrong way down a street. You might then decide to turn around in the middle of the street. This kind of a turn is called a turnabout.

A turnabout can be a U-turn.

A turnabout also can be made by a set of forward and backward movements. A turnabout also can be made by making forward and backward moves while turning the steering wheel all the way to the left and then to the right.

A turnabout may not be made where:

- a sign is posted saying you may not make a U-turn;

- on a curve;

- near the top of a hill;

- any place where the driver cannot see, or be seen, for at least 500 feet.

Remember that you travel about 90 feet in just 1 second when you are driving at 60 mph. The person driving behind you needs to know that you are planning to make a turn. Be alert to how much time the person behind you needs to prepare for your turn.

In the city, it is often easier and safer to drive around the block than try to make a turnabout. This is very true when going around the block places you at a corner with traffic signal lights. The traffic signal lights will help you to cross a busy street safely.

Drive Smart!

Directions: Read each sentence. Put an X in the box in front of the words that best answer the question or finish the sentence.

1. The hand signal for a right turn is given by

   ☐ pointing your arm and hand downward.

   ☐ pointing your arm and hand upward.

   ☐ pointing your arm and hand straight out.

2. When you want to make a turn in the city, you must signal at least _____ before you make the turn.

   ☐ 500 feet   ☐ 400 feet

   ☐ 200 feet   ☐ 100 feet

3. You are driving in the left lane on a four-lane street. You stop for a red traffic signal. You find that this is where you want to turn. What should you do?

   ☐ Be careful, but make the turn anyway.

   ☐ Turn left, and go around the block.

   ☐ Drive ahead when traffic goes, signal, and move into the right lane for a right turn.

   ☐ Signal right, and turn in front of traffic in the right lane.

4. You are driving 25 mph on a city street. There are no traffic signals or stop signs on the street. As you come near a corner, you see that a pedestrian will reach the crosswalk about the same time that you do. Who has the right of way?

    ☐ you

    ☐ the pedestrian

    ☐ No one has right of way; it must be given.

5. You are driving on a city street. You come to a corner where you want to turn left. There is an oncoming car near the corner and a pedestrian crossing the street to your left. Who has the right-of-way?

    ☐ to you

    ☐ to the driver of the oncoming car

    ☐ to the pedestrian

    ☐ to the pedestrian and the oncoming car

CHAPTER 8: Speed Limits

Before you read, you should know that:

▶ **maximum** (MAKS-ih-mum) **speed** is the fastest speed you are allowed to travel;

▶ **minimum** (MIN-ih-mum) **speed** is the slowest speed you are allowed to travel;

▶ a **zone** (ZOHN) is a special area;

▶ a **speed limit** is the speed you may by law travel on a street;

▶ a **construction** (con-STRUK-shun) **zone** is a place where road work is taking place.

▼ A speed limit is the speed you may travel by law on a street. Maximum and minimum speeds are given for times when the road is safe.

⚡**Maximum** and **minimum** speeds are given for times when the road is safe. A safe road is one that is dry and smooth. A safe road also is one where there is not more traffic than the road was meant to have at one time.

After reading this chapter, you should be able to:

▶ give the **speed limits** for city and highway driving;

▶ tell what following distance (DIS-tans) means;

▶ tell when you must change your following distance.

PASS THAT TEST !

Speed Law

The UVC suggests two speed limits. One limit is 30 mph. This speed is suggested for driving on city streets. A slower speed is suggested in the city because of the greater risk of a crash. Driving at a slower speed in the city makes for safer driving.

The other speed suggested by the UVC is 55 mph. This speed is suggested for driving on roads in rural (ROO-ral) areas. Rural areas are places beyond the city. On such roads, the driver can often see more of what is ahead. The driver can adjust or fix the driving speed as needed.

Federal law, or law that govern all the country, permits a maximum speed of 65 mph on special highways. These highways are part of the Interstate (IN-ter-stayt) Highway System (SIS-tem).

Interstate means that these roads pass across a number of states. Some cross the United States from the East Coast to the West Coast. Other interstate highways cross the country from north to south.

Interstate highways are marked by a special sign. The sign looks like a shield (SHEELD).

CHECK YOUR STATE MANUAL Most states have a speed limit of 65 mph on their interstate highways. A number of states have voted to keep the speed limit at 55 mph. These states are mostly in the northeast part of the country. The states have done this because of the great number of vehicles using the roads. With more vehicles, there is a greater risk of having a serious crash.

There are some states with a 65 mph interstate speed that, in places, drop the speed to 55 mph. The speed must drop to 55 mph anytime the highway passes across or near a city of 50,000 or more people.

Some states use a Basic Speed Law. This law says that a driver look at the conditions (con-DIH-shunz) for driving. Is it raining? Is the road covered with snow? Is the road in good condition? Is the vehicle safe to drive at a faster speed? Based on these conditions, the driver must then decides what is a safe speed.

Most states have speed limits for special areas. These would be:
- parks;
- a school **zone;**
- business areas;
- road repair and **construction** (con-STRUK-shun) **zones.**

The state of Connecticut passed the first speed limit law in 1901. The law said drivers could drive at 12 mph in the city. They could drive 15 mph in rural areas.

About 800 people are killed in crashes in road construction zones each year. Of these 800, about 120 are persons working on the road.

PASS THAT TEST !

Following Distance

Following distance (DIS-tans) is the distance between you and the vehicle in front of you. The UVC says that you should make sure your following distance is a safe distance.

PASS THAT TEST

Your following distance changes as the driving conditions change. These are some of the things you should watch for:

- the speed of your vehicle;
- the speed of the other vehicles;
- the number of vehicles around you;
- the condition of the road;
- weather (WEH-ther) conditions;
- how well you can see.

Sometimes, you may have to stop suddenly. Sometimes, traffic stops quickly. You must always have plenty of room between you and the vehicle ahead of you to let you stop safely.

Something may happen that causes you to lose your safe following distance. If this happens, you need to watch for a place to steer. Often, it takes less time to steer into a safe area than to stop. For most people, this is true at speeds over 25 mph to 30 mph.

There is a special following distance for fire trucks. The law says that drivers must stay at least 500 feet in back of a fire truck. This is about the same distance as one city block.

Some state laws say that you must keep a minimum following distance of one car length for every 10 mph. For example, at 40 mph you must have a following distance of four car lengths. A car length is equal to about 15 feet. At 40 mph this is 60 feet. Sixty feet is equal to the distance you will travel in one second at 40 mph. More time than this is often needed in an emergency situation.

Other states have laws that say you must have a following distance of 2 to 3 seconds. For example, in 1 second at 40 mph, you travel about 60 feet. This means that with a 2 to 3 second following distance, you are 120 feet to 180 feet behind the vehicle ahead of you.

This distance lets you see more of what is ahead of you. It also gives you more time to steer or brake if the need arises.

▲ Some states have laws that say you must have a following distance of two or three seconds.

Drive Smart!

Directions: Fill in the blank with the correct number.

For the state in which you live:

1. the maximum speed limit on rural interstate highways is _____ mph.

2. the maximum speed limit on streets in cities is _____ mph.

3. the speed limit in school zones in _____ mph.

4. the speed limit in highway construction areas is _____ mph.

5. a driver must try to have a following distance of at least

_____.

▲ In 20 percent of all crashes, a following vehicle crashes into the vehicle ahead.

Directions: Read each situation. Then write the answer to the questions at the end of each situation.

1. You are behind a truck traveling at a speed of 50 mph on a two-lane highway. You are following the truck at a distance of five car lengths (75 feet). A friend riding with you says you are too close to the truck.

   What do you think? Why?

   _____

   _____

   _____

   _____

   _____

2. You are behind a car traveling at 53 mph on a two lane road. The speed limit on the road is 55 mph. You increase your speed to 65 mph to pass the car. A friend riding with you says that what you did was against the speed-limit law.

   What do you think? Why?

   _____

   _____

   _____

   _____

   _____

CHAPTER 9: Stopping, Parking, Backing

Before you read, you should know that:

▶ to **stand a vehicle** means when the driver stays in the vehicle while it is stopped for a short time;

▶ a **traffic control device** (deh-VYS) is a something used to guide, warn, or direct drivers;

▶ to **yield** means to let someone go first, to give the right-of-way;

▶ **parallel** (PAR-ah-lel) means to park in line with something, such as a curb or road edge.

After reading this chapter, you should be able to:

▶ tell how you stop at stop signs and railroad crossings;

▶ tell about ten places you may not park or **stand a vehicle;**

▶ tell what you should watch for when backing a vehicle.

⚡ All drivers must obey (oh-BAY) or do what a **traffic control device** tells them to do. A driver does not have to obey a traffic control device when a police officer says to do something else.

Stopping

You must stop when you see a stop sign. Here is what you must do when you see a stop sign:

• stop at the stop sign or the clearly marked stop line;

• if there is no stop line, stop before the crosswalk;

• if there is no crosswalk, stop near the intersection where you can see the traffic.

▲ You must stop when you see a stop sign.

After stopping, you must **yield** the right-of-way to any vehicle in the intersection. You also must yield the right-of-way to any vehicle close enough to the intersection to be a danger to you.

Drivers stopped for a stop sign must yield the right-of-way to any pedestrian in the crosswalk.

Every driver exiting or leaving from an alley, building, private road, or driveway must stop before driving onto a sidewalk. If there is no sidewalk, the stop must be made near the street where traffic can be seen.

PASS THAT TEST !

Yielding

Every driver coming to a yield right-of-way sign must slow to a safe speed. The driver must be ready to stop.

The driver must stop if it is not safe to drive into traffic. The driver may enter the intersection (IN-ter-sek-shun) only when it is safe to do so. An intersection is where two roads cross. Drive into traffic when the traffic clears.

PASS THAT TEST !

Railroad Crossings

You must stop at a railroad crossing when you see a train coming. You must stop at a railroad crossing when a train coming toward you sounds its horn or whistle. Your stop cannot be closer than 15 feet from the closest train track. But your stop must be made within 50 feet of the closest train track.

You also must stop at a railroad crossing when:

- a flashing red signal warns you that a train is coming;

- the crossing gate is down;

- a flagger warns you that a train is coming.

▲ You must stop at a railroad crossing no closer than 15 feet from the closest train track.

WATCH OUT !

No driver may drive a vehicle around or under any railroad crossing gate when the gate is closed. No driver may drive a vehicle around or under a crossing gate when it is being opened or closed.

Crash records show that one of the leading causes of death at railroad crossings is driving around the end of crossing gates that are down to stop traffic for an oncoming train.

PASS THAT TEST !

Parking

Parking a vehicle means to stop and leave a vehicle at the same place for a while. Every vehicle parked on a road must be parked **parallel** to the curb or edge of the road. It must be faced in the same direction (dih-

REK-shun) or lined up in the same way as the traffic. The wheels of the vehicle must be within 12 inches of the curb or edge of the road.

When a vehicle is parked on a flat surface, the front wheels must be turned to the right. This is true when the vehicle is facing downhill where there is a curb. This also is true when the vehicle is facing uphill where there is no curb.

Sometimes, you must park on the roadway. When this happens, you must:

- park so traffic can drive around your vehicle;

- park where all other drivers can see your vehicle from a distance of at least 200 feet away.

These rules do not apply if something happens to your vehicle and you cannot move it. In a time like this, you must warn other drivers that your vehicle is stopped in the roadway.

▲ Sometimes, when parking on the roadway, you must park where all other drivers can see your vehicle.

WATCH OUT !

You may not park, stand, or leave a vehicle in the following places:
- on a road when it is possible to place the vehicle off the road;
- on the road side of any other vehicle (double park);
- on a sidewalk or crosswalk;
- within an intersection;
- on any bridge or within any tunnel;
- on any railroad track;
- on any highway;
- on the median of a divided highway;
- in a parking space set aside for disabled drivers;
- where no-stopping signs are posted;
- in front of a driveway;
- within 15 feet of a fire hydrant (HI-drant);
- within 20 feet of an intersection;
- within 30 feet of a stop sign, yield sign, flashing signal or traffic control signal located beside the road;
- within 20 feet of a fire station driveway;
- within 75 feet on the other side of the street from a fire station;
- within 50 feet of a railroad crossing.

DID YOU KNOW?

People may angle park in parking lots. Drivers may not angle park in most towns and cities. Drivers may angle park in some places. Yet, this is only after a study has been done on how the angle parking will affect the safety of highway users.

▲ Backing means moving a vehicle in reverse. Before backing, check carefully behind the vehicle for children or objects.

DID YOU KNOW?

Backing is one of the leading causes of traffic deaths of children under 5 years of age. Most such deaths happen in the family driveway or at the curb in front of the home. In most cases, the driver is a family member or a friend.

Drive Smart!

Directions: Read each situation. Then write what you would do. Give a reason for your answer.

1. **Situation:** You have stopped at a stop sign. You want to go across the corner or across the street. You move up to the curb line to check traffic. There are cars coming from both your right and left. They are not quite a half block away. What should you do? Why?

   _____

   _____

   _____

2. **Situation:** You are coming to an intersection. You see a Yield sign on your street. Your view of the cross street is blocked by shrubs and trees. What should you do? Why?

   _____

   _____

   _____

3. **Situation:** You are coming to a railroad crossing. As you get close to the railroad tracks, the red lights start to flash. The gates start to come down. You look both ways but do not see a train coming. What should you do? Why?

   _____

   _____

   _____

4. **Situation:** You car is parked in the driveway. There is no room to turn around. You will have to back out of the driveway and into the street. What should you do? Why?

_____

_____

_____

_____

5. **Situation:** You are going to park parallel to a curb facing uphill. How many inches from the curb does the law say you should be? Which way should you turn the front wheels of your vehicle? Why?

_____

_____

_____

_____

Section 3 Review   MOVING IN TRAFFIC

Directions: These questions come from Chapters 4 - 9. You may look back to these chapters if you need help in choosing the correct answer. Remember to read each sentence carefully. Then write X beside the answer you choose.

CHAPTER 4 Driving on the Right Side of the Road

1. You may drive to the left of a solid yellow center line, on your side of the road, when
    ___   a.   you are coming to a curve.
    ___   b.   you are passing another vehicle.
    ___   c.   a police officer directs you to do so.
    ___   d.   you are near the top of a hill.

CHAPTER 5 Passing

1. After passing a vehicle you should not steer back into your lane until
    ___   a.   you can see the front of the vehicle you are passing in your rear view mirror.
    ___   b.   you can see the front of the vehicle when you turn your head to the right.
    ___   c.   you are 400 feet ahead of the vehicle.
    ___   d.   the driver you are passing flashes his lights.

2. You may pass a school bus that is stopped, on your side of the road, with its lights flashing
    ___   a.   only if you stop first and then drive slowly past it.
    ___   b.   only if children are getting on, but not off the bus.
    ___   c.   only when directed to do so by the driver or a police officer.
    ___   d.   only if you are very careful.

3. You may pass another vehicle on the right if
    ___   a.   you sound your horn first.
    ___   b.   you first signal a move to the right.
    ___   c.   the vehicle ahead stops for a pedestrian.
    ___   d.   the road has two or more lanes of traffic moving in the same way.

4. When you are being passed by another vehicle, you should
    ___   a.   steer to the left side of your lane and slow down a little.
    ___   b.   steer to the right side of your lane and speed up a little.
    ___   c.   steer to the right side of your lane, keep a steady speed, but be ready to slow.
    ___   d.   steer to the left side of your lane, keep a steady speed, but be ready to slow.

CHAPTER 6 Right-of-Way

1. At an intersection where there are no traffic control devices, and two or more vehicles come to the intersection at the same time
    ___   a.   the vehicle on the right should be given the right-of-way.
    ___   b.   the vehicle on the left should be given the right-of-way.
    ___   c.   the first vehicle into the intersection has the right-of-way.
    ___   d.   the first driver who flashes his or her lights has the right-of-way.

2. You are driving on a two-lane road, which of the following should yield right-of-way to you at an intersection?
    ___   a.   an ambulance   ___ b.   a police car
    ___   c.   a pedestrian   ___   d.   a car turning left

CHAPTER 7 Turning and Lane Changes

1. When you want to make a left or right turn in the city, you must signal at least how far before making the turn?
    ___   a.   100 feet   ___   b.   150 feet
    ___   c.   200 feet   ___   d.   Other: _____ feet

2. When making a left turn onto a one-way street, you must turn from the farthest left lane or marked turn lane(s) into
  ___ a. the farthest right lane.
  ___ b. the nearest left travel lane.
  ___ c. no lane, you may not turn left onto a one-way street.

3. The hand signal for a right turn is given by holding the left arm and hand
  ___ a. straight out from the left side of the vehicle.
  ___ b. out and down from the left side of the vehicle.
  ___ c. out and up from the left side of the vehicle.

CHAPTER 8 Speed Limits

1. You are driving in a rural area in your home state. Unless otherwise posted, the maximum speed limit for cars is
  ___ a. 50 miles per hour.   ___ b. 55 miles per hour.
  ___ c. 60 miles per hour.   ___ d. 65 miles per hour.

2. There is a maximum speed limit of 65 and a minimum speed limit of 45 mph posted on a highway. Weather and road conditions are good and your vehicle is running well. You should
  ___ a. drive 40 mph.
  ___ b. go no slower than 45 nor faster than 65 mph.
  ___ c. drive no faster than 70 mph.
  ___ d. drive at a speed at which you feel comfortable.

3. In the state in which you live, the law requires that under good road and weather conditions, when following another vehicle you must
  ___ a. allow at least one car length per each ten miles per hour.
  ___ b. allow at least two seconds betwen your vehicle and the vehicle ahead.
  ___ c. always follow at a safe distance.
  ___ d. follow the vehicle ahead at a distance that feels comfortable.

CHAPTER 9 Stopping, Parking, Backing

1. When approaching an intersection controlled by a stop sign and stop line, a driver
  ___ a. must slow and check traffic before making a turn.
  ___ b. may drive to the road edge without stopping at the stop line.
  ___ c. must stop only if vehicles are crossing the intersection.
  ___ d. must stop at the stop line, and go only when it is safe to do so.

2. When parking a vehicle at a curb, facing down the hill, the front wheels must be
  ___ a. pointed straight ahead and within 12 inches of the curb.
  ___ b. pointed toward the street with the back of the tire against the curb.
  ___ c. pointed toward the curb with the front of the tire against the curb.
  ___ d. doesn't matter which the way the tires point as long as you are within 12 inches of the curb.

3. You are coming to a railroad crossing. There are no crossing gates, but the red signal lights start to flash. You should
  ___ a. keep going if you don't see a train.
  ___ b. stop and then cross if you don't see a train.
  ___ c. step on the accelerator, you can beat the train.
  ___ d. stop and wait for the train unless a flagger directs you to cross.

SECTION 4: VEHICLE SAFETY LAWS

CHECK YOUR STATE MANUAL
All motor vehicles registered in a state shall be checked for safety once each year. All safe vehicles will be given a paper stating that the vehicle is safe.

Each state handles this law in its own way. Check your state law to see how it is handled in your town or city.

No one may drive a vehicle on any highway unless the vehicle is in safe working order. The vehicle must not be a danger to the driver, to the people riding in the vehicle or to any other person or property.

CHAPTER 10: Lights, Mirrors, and Windshields

Before you read, you should know that:

- a **headlight** is one of two or four lights on the front of a vehicle;

- a **brake light** is a red light on the back of a vehicle that lights up when the driver steps on the brake pedal;

- **parking lights** are the two small orange lights on the front of a vehicle and the two red lights on the back of a vehicle;

- a **windshield** (WIND-sheeld) is the large area of glass on the front of a vehicle.

After reading this chapter, you should be able to:

- tell about three kinds of lights;

- tell where a vehicle's mirrors should be;

- tell how to have a clear view of the road.

▲ A headlight is one of two or four lights on the front of a vehicle.

▼ The purpose of headlights is to light up the road ahead when it is dark.

PASS THAT TEST !

Headlights

Every vehicle must have at least two headlights. At least one **headlight** must be on each side of the front of the vehicle. The purpose of headlights is to light up the road ahead when it is dark.

Headlights must be turned on from one half hour after sunset to one half hour before sunrise. Headlights also must be used when weather makes it hard to see clearly persons and vehicles two city blocks away (1,000 feet). The same distance is true for any other conditions that make it hard to see clearly.

A driver must dim the headlights 500 feet before an oncoming vehicle. Also, a driver must dim the headlights within 300 feet of the vehicle ahead.

Spotlights

A vehicle may have two spotlights. The spotlights must be aimed in such a way that the light does not strike the windshield of other vehicles. The light also may not strike any windows, mirrors, or people in other vehicles.

Brake and Other Lights

Every vehicle must have at least two **brake lights** on the rear, or back, of the vehicle. The purpose of brake lights is to tell drivers behind that you are stopping or slowing. Brake lights are red.

All cars made after January 1, 1953 also must have flashing turn signal lights. Flashing turn-signal lights are red or yellow.

All vehicles must have at least two taillights (TAYL-lyts). Red taillights come on when you turn on your headlights or parking lights.

All vehicles have white backup lights. These lights come on when you put your vehicle in reverse to backup.

You also must have a license plate light. This light is above your license plate. It comes on when you turn on your headlights. It's purpose is for the license plate to be easily seen at night.

Parking Lights

Every vehicle must have **parking lights.** Parking lights are not for lighting the road while you are driving. They are to warn other drivers that your vehicle is parked or stopped along the highway.

Parking lights must be used from one half hour after sunset to one half hour before sunrise. The headlights of a parked vehicle must be dimmed when parked.

Emergency Lights

Emergency lights also are called **hazard** (HAH-zard), or danger, warning lights. Emergency lights also may be called emergency flashers. Emergency lights make all four turn-signal lights flash at the same time.

Emergency lights must be used when:

- the vehicle is stopped within a business district where it is not legal to park;

- the vehicle is stopped to let people get out of or into the vehicle;

- making a stop due to changes in the traffic flow;

- making a stop when told to do so by a police officer.

Emergency lights may be used when:

- you wish to warn drivers behind you of a traffic hazard ahead;

- you wish to signal that your own vehicle is a hazard.

CHECK YOUR STATE MANUAL Several states have passed laws that say headlights must be on anytime the **windshield** wipers are being used.

▲ Every vehicle must have at least two brake lights on the rear of the vehicle.

DID YOU KNOW?

Another use for lights is to warn you have something that extends out the sides or four feet beyond the rear of your vehicle.

- At night: Use one red light on each side of a load to show how far the load extends beyond your vehicle. You also must have two red reflectors (re-FLEK-tors) to show how wide the load is.

- During the day: Red flags no smaller than 12 inches wide are used in place of the red lights and reflectors.

▲ Every vehicle must have a mirror mounted on the left side to give the driver a rear view.

▼ Every vehicle must have a second mirror.

PASS THAT TEST !

Mirrors

Every vehicle must have a mirror mounted on the left side of the vehicle. The mirror must give the driver a view of the road behind the vehicle. This view is called a rear view.

Every vehicle must have a second mirror. The second mirror may be mounted on the inside of the vehicle. If mounted inside, the mirror must be about in the center of the vehicle. It must be mounted toward the top of the front windshield.

A second mirror may be mounted on the right side of the vehicle. If mounted here, it must be set up so that it gives the driver a rear view of the road.

WATCH OUT !

Even when using mirrors, you will still have blind spots. Blind spots are areas of the road that you cannot see in the mirror. Because of this, always check your mirrors AND over your shoulder before changing lanes.

PASS THAT TEST !

Windshields

A federal standard (STAN-dard), or guide for all states in the country, says how dark the glass should be for the windshield on vehicles. There also is a federal standard for the darkness of glass on side windows.

Every vehicle must have windshield wipers to clean water and snow from the glass. The wipers must be in good working condition at all times.

DID YOU KNOW?

It is not a law but a good idea when driving to check the mirrors any time you think you may have to change speed or position (po-SIH-shun).

It also is a good idea to check the mirrors when driving down a long, steep hill. In a time like this, you are checking for trucks that have lost their brakes. In such a situation, steer off the road. Stop to let the truck pass.

WATCH OUT !

No one may drive a vehicle with anything stuck to the front windshield that keeps the driver from having a clear view of the road. A clear view means that the driver does not have to look around anything on the car in order to see the road.

No one may drive a vehicle with anything stuck to any window on the vehicle that keeps the driver from having a clear view of the road.

No one may hang anything inside a vehicle that keeps the driver from having a clear view of the road.

Drive Smart!

Directions: Read each sentence. If the sentence is true or correct, put an X in the TRUE box. If the sentence if not true, put an X in the FALSE box. Rewrite each false sentence to make it true.

CHECK YOUR STATE MANUAL Some states permit a darker glass in the front side windows. This darker glass makes it harder to see things at night. In some states, this darker glass is against the law.

1. The state in which you live says that headlights must be on from one half hour after sunset to one half hour before sunrise.

   TRUE ☐   FALSE ☐

   _____

   _____

2. The state in which your live says that a driver must dim the headlights at least 500 feet from an oncoming vehicle.

   TRUE ☐   FALSE ☐

   _____

   _____

3. A vehicle must have at least three mirrors.

   TRUE ☐   FALSE ☐

   _____

   _____

4. The state in which you live says that you may have a sticker on the center of your windshield.

   TRUE ☐   FALSE ☐

   _____

   _____

5. Before changing lanes, always check your mirrors and over your shoulder.

   TRUE ☐   FALSE ☐

   _____

   _____

CHAPTER 11: Brakes, Tires, and Horns

▼ Every vehicle must have brakes that are in good working condition.

Before you read, you should know that:

▶ a brake is that part of the vehicle that lets the driver bring the vehicle to a stop;

▶ a parking brake (emergency brake) is that part of the brake system that holds a vehicle in place after it has been stopped;

▶ tread is that part of a tire that touches the road;

▶ warning devices are things such as horns and sirens used to alert drivers and other road users.

After reading this chapter, you should be able to:

▶ tell when the **brakes** in a vehicle are used;

▶ tell what a safe tire means;

▶ tell which warning devices a vehicle may have.

PASS THAT TEST !

Brakes

Every vehicle must have brakes that are in good working condition. The brakes on a car traveling 20 mph must be able to bring the car to a stop in 40 feet on a dry, clean road.

DID YOU KNOW?

You do not want to lock the brakes when stopping. When you press the brake pedal too hard, the tires slide. When the tires slide, you cannot steer.

To keep from locking the brakes, keep your heel on the floor. Squeeze (skweez) down firmly on the brake pedal with your toes. This way of braking also works better on wet, snow or ice covered roads.

PASS THAT TEST !

Parking Brake

Every vehicle also must have a **parking brake.** The parking brake must be able to hold the vehicle when it is parked. A parking brake also must be able to hold a vehicle parked on a clean, dry hill road.

DID YOU KNOW?

For a parking brake to work well the road must be dry and hard. Parking brakes do not work well on gravel roads. A parking brake also does not work well when the road has ice or snow on it.

PASS THAT TEST !

Tires

Every vehicle driven on a road must have tires that are in safe operating (OP-er-ay-ting) condition. Safe operation condition means no cuts, bruises (BROO-zez), or bulges. By law, the tires must have at least 2/32 (1/16) of an inch of **tread.** This is called tread depth.

The purpose of tire tread is to cool the tire. Tire tread also wipes away water or sand. This gives the tire a better grip on the road.

The tires should have proper tire pressure (PREH-shur). Proper tire **pressure** better tire wear and car control. Check your owner's manual to find the correct pressure for your tires. For the best control, add pressure suggested for highway driving.

PASS THAT TEST !

Horns

A horn is a **warning device.** Other warning devices are sirens (SY-rens), whistles, and bells.

Every vehicle must have a horn that works. The horn must be able to make a sound loud enough to be heard at least 200 feet away.

A vehicle may have a theft alarm device. A theft alarm device lets the vehicle owner know when someone is breaking into the vehicle. A theft alarm device may use a whistle, bell, or horn.

Emergency vehicles, such as police cars and ambulances (AM-byoo-lan-sez), use warning devices. The warning devices used on emergency vehicles are sirens, whistles, or bells.

The warning device must have a sound that can be heard at least 500 feet away. Emergency vehicles may only use warning devices when there is an emergency.

▲ You should check your tire tread depth once each week.

WATCH OUT !

Theft alarm devices may not use sirens.

Theft alarm devices may not be used as normal warning devices. This means that the sound given off by a theft alarm device may only be used when someone is breaking into the vehicle. Warning sounds given off by theft alarm devices may not be used during driving.

▲ Every vehicle must have a horn that works.

Drive Smart!

Directions: Read each sentence. Put an X in the box next to the words that best finish the sentence.

1. At a speed of 20 mph, the brakes on a car must be able to stop the car in

   ☐ 10 feet.
   ☐ 20 feet.
   ☐ 30 feet.
   ☐ 40 feet.

2. A parking brake is to be used

   ☐ to stop your car whenever you drive.
   ☐ in an emergency.
   ☐ to hold the car in place when it is parked.
   ☐ as little as possible.

3. To be legal, a tire must have at least

   ☐ some tread.
   ☐ no white marks.
   ☐ 1/32 of an inch of tread.
   ☐ 2/32 of an inch of tread.

4. A tire with 2/32 of an inch of tread is safe to use

   ☐ on any road surface.
   ☐ on clean, dry roads.
   ☐ only on roads with gravel.
   ☐ on snow-covered roads.

5. A theft alarm may use

   ☐ a siren sound.
   ☐ a whistle sound.
   ☐ a siren and bells.
   ☐ only bells.

Hints to Help You Pass that Test!

Matching

Matching questions ask you to look at a picture or read a phrase. You then must match that picture or phrase with something that means the same thing. You will find matching questions in this book. Here are some hints on how to handle matching questions.

Hint # 1

Read the directions (dy-REK-shuns) carefully. Find out if you are to look for only one answer.

Which sentence matches the picture? Note that you are being asked for only one match.

    a. tells you to drive faster
    b. tells you to turn right
    c. tells you to stop
    d. tells you to slow down

Do the easiest matches first. This will save you time so you are sure to finish the test. Mark the questions you are not sure of as you work quickly. Then, go back to the matching questions that gave you trouble.

Hint # 2

On questions that match phrases or groups of words, try to find a way in which two phrases connect.

Directions: Draw lines to correctly match these phrases.

left turn lane	traffic travels only one way
one-way street	how fast you may drive
speed limit	a lane directing your turn
crossing the intersection	go across a travel path

Directions: Match the phrase to make a true sentence.

    ____ 1. When coming to an intersection   a. have 55 mph speed limits.
    ____ 2. Most rural roads   b. you should stop.
    ____ 3. Most interstate highways   c. watch for control devices.
    ____ 4. A flashing red light means   d. have 65 mph speed limits.

Section 4 Review   VEHICLE SAFETY LAWS

Directions: These questions come from Chapters 10 and 11. You may look back to these chapters if you need help in choosing the correct answer. Remember to read each sentence carefully. Then write X beside the answer you choose.

CHAPTER 10 Lights, Mirrors, and Windshields

1. A driver must dim the headlights at least how many feet from an oncoming vehicle?
   ___ a. 150 feet   ___ b. 350 fee
   ___ c. 500 feet   ___ d. Other

2 A driver must dim the headlights at least how far behind the vehicle ahead?
   ___ a. 100 feet   ___ b. 200 feet
   ___ c. 300 feet   ___ d. Other

3. A driver must turn on the headlights of a vehicle
   ___ a. one half hour before sunset.
   ___ b. at sunset.
   ___ c. one half hour after sunset.
   ___ d. any time that visibility is limited to 1000 feet or less.

4. Every car must have at least two (2) mirrors to let the driver see the rear.
   ___ True
   ___ False

5. Every new vehicle must be equipped with turn indicator lights on both the front and rear.
   ___ True
   ___ False

CHAPTER 11 Brakes, Tires, and Horns

1. The parking brake on a car is meant to be used
   ___ a. to stop your car when driving in traffic.
   ___ b. in an emergency.
   ___ c. to hold the car in place when it is parked.
   ___ d. as little as possible.

2. To be legal a tire must have at least
   ___ a. some tread in the middle of the tire.
   ___ b. at least 2/32 inch of tread at all points on the tire.
   ___ c. at least 2/16 inch of tread at all points on the tire.
   ___ d. 1/4 inch of tread.

3. A car's horn must be loud enough so that it can be heard at a distance of at least
   ___ a. 100 feet.   ___ b. 200 feet.
   ___ c. 300 feet.   ___ d. 400 feet.

The People's Publishing Group, Inc.:*Studying for a Driver's License*

SECTION 5:   ROAD MARKINGS

⚡ Road markings tell drivers what they may or may not do. In some cases, road markings tell drivers what they must do.

CHAPTER 12: White Road Markings

Before you read, you should know that:

▶ an **interchange entrance** (EN-trans) **ramp** is a special one-way road that takes vehicles onto a high-speed roadway;

▶ an **interchange exit** (EKS-it) **ramp** is a special one-way road that takes vehicles off a high-speed roadway;

▶ a **high speed roadway** is a highway, freeway, or other road with limited access (AK-ses);

▶ **limited access** means that drivers can get on or off the road only at an interchange (IN-ter-chanj);

▶ an **interchange** takes the place of an intersection and lets vehicles move from one road to another by changing speed and place to move smoothly into traffic without stopping;

▶ **pavement** (PAYV-ment) is the hard surface of a road.

After reading this chapter, you should be able to:

▶ tell where a broken white line is used;

▶ tell where a solid while line is used;

▶ tell how two other white road markings are used.

PASS THAT TEST !

Broken White Lane Lines

Broken white lane lines are used to separate (SEP-ah-rayt),or divide, traffic moving in the same way, or direction. You may drive across a broken white line to move to another lane of traffic. Before moving to another lane, you must make sure the move can be made safely.

◀ Broken white lines are used to separate traffic moving in the same direction.

Solid White Lane Lines

Solid white lines are used to mark the right edge of a road. At times, they are used to separate traffic moving in the same direction.

Here are other places where you will find solid white lines:

- at intersections;
- in places where the road is being repaired or built;
- to mark special right- or left-turn lanes;
- at an **interchange entrance** or **interchange exit.**

Solid white lines here help drivers move away from or onto a **high-speed roadway.** They help drivers make their moves easier and with greater safety.

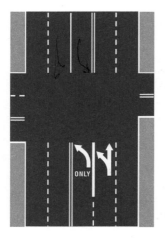

▲ Solid white lines mark special right- or left-turn lanes.

▲ At an interchange or exit, solid white lines help drivers move away
▼ from or onto a high-speed road.

Even when traffic laws say you may cross a solid white lane line, it is still very unsafe to cross. A driver who is in a crash because of crossing a solid white lane line often will get a ticket. The ticket will likely be for "Making an Improper (im-PROP-er) Lane Change." Used here, **improper** means the move was unsafe.

Solid White Lines That Cross Lane Lines

There are places where solid white lines cross traffic lanes. Drivers must watch for and be ready to stop when a solid white line crosses the lane in which they are driving. Pedestrians and people riding bicycles also must watch for solid white lines and act as directed by these lines.

A solid white line across a traffic lane often is used with a stop sign. This line shows a driver where to stop.

Two white lines are used to mark pedestrian crosswalks. The white lines tell pedestrians where to walk. Drivers must yield the right-of-way to pedestrians crossing a street in the marked crosswalk.

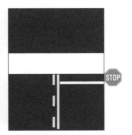

◀ Solid white lines across a traffic lane show a driver where to stop. It is often used with a stop sign.

▼ Two white lines mark pedestrian crosswalks. They tell people where to walk. Drivers must yield right-of-way.

▲ Drivers must follow the direction of the arrow.

Other Pavement Markings

As drivers get close to an intersection, they often will see white arrows painted on the pavement. The arrows may point left, right, or straight ahead. Before drivers get to the arrow marking, they also will see the word **ONLY** painted on the pavement.

Sometimes, an arrow will point straight ahead and to the left.

Other times, the arrow may point straight ahead and to the right.

When an arrow is painted on the pavement, drivers in that lane must go in the direction the arrow points. A driver who does not go where the arrow points is guilty (GIL-tee) of improper lane use. The driver may get a ticket. The driver may have to pay a fine.

At times, a traffic lane will be marked with a restricted lane marking. Sometimes, a restricted-lane (re-STRIK-ted) marking will limit use of a traffic lane to certain kinds of vehicles. Sometimes, the lane may be used only by buses or car pools. (A car pool is a group of people riding together to or from work in a car or van.)

Other times, restricted lanes can be used only by vehicles making certain moves.

As you drive, you will sometime see two **R**'s with a large **X** plus two solid white lines on the **pavement.** These markings warn drivers of a railroad crossing.

At times, restricted lane markings are used. Restricted-lane markings limit, or restrict, the use of a lane to certain vehicles. Restricted-lane markings also are used to restrict the moves a driver may make while driving in a certain lane.

▲ Restricted lane marking.

Drive Smart!

Directions: Read each situation. If the last sentence of the situation is true, or correct, put an X in the TRUE box. If the last sentence is false, put an X in the FALSE box. Rewrite each false sentence to make it true.

1. You are driving on a four-lane road. The lanes are marked with broken white lines. It is OK to pass a vehicle ahead of you when it is safe to do so.

   TRUE ☐   FALSE ☐

   _____

   _____

   _____

2. Sold white lane lines are used on road edges and at intersections. Solid white lane lines also are used at interchange exits, to mark special right-turn lanes, and to divide two lanes of traffic moving in the same direction.

   TRUE ☐   FALSE ☐

   _____

   _____

   _____

3. You are coming to an intersection. You want to go straight across. Ahead in your lane, you see the word **ONLY** and a white arrow pointing to the right. It is OK for you to go straight.

   TRUE ☐   FALSE ☐

   _____

   _____

   _____

4. You are coming to a stop sign. There is a solid white line across your lane in line with the stop sign. It is OK for you to go all the way to the curb before you stop.

TRUE ☐   FALSE ☐

_____

_____

_____

_____

5. It is seven o'clock in the morning. You are driving to work. There is no one else in the car with you. On the pavement, you see a restricted-lane sign that says, "Buses and Car Pools Only, 6:30 A.M. to 9 A.M." You will get a ticket if you stay in the lane.

TRUE ☐   FALSE ☐

_____

_____

_____

_____

CHAPTER 13: Yellow Road Markings

Before you read, you should know that:

▶ a **center line** is the line that divides traffic going in different or opposite (OP-poh-sit) ways;

▶ a **two-lane road** is a road with two lanes of traffic, one lane of traffic moving in one direction and the other lane of traffic moving in the opposite direction.

DID YOU KNOW?

Sometimes, on very narrow two-lane roads, center lines are marked with a single yellow line. This happens most often on country (KUN-tree) roads or in mountain (MOUN-ten) areas. A single yellow center line also may be seen on narrow roads that run beside a river or lake.

After reading this chapter, you will be able to:

▶ tell where a broken yellow line is used;

▶ tell where a solid yellow line is used;

▶ tell how two yellow lines let you know when you may pass a vehicle.

⚡ Yellow lane lines are used to separate traffic moving in opposite directions. They are used to mark the left edge of a divided road. Yellow lane lines also may be used to mark a left-turn bay.

Two solid yellow lines mean it ▼ is not legal to pass.

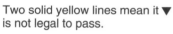

PASS THAT TEST !

Broken Yellow Lane Line

The **center line** of a **two-lane road** often is marked by a broken yellow lane line. The broken yellow line tells the driver that it is legal to pass a slower vehicle. As a driver, you must decide if it is safe to pass.

▲ A broken yellow lane line tells the driver it is legal to pass.

PASS THAT TEST !

Two Solid Yellow Lane Lines

The center line of a road with two or more lanes may be marked with two solid yellow lane lines. Two solid yellow lines means that it is not legal for a driver to pass another vehicle. This law is true for drivers going in either direction.

Solid yellow lines also may be used to mark protected left-turn lanes. This happens on roads with two or more lanes of traffic going in the same direction.

One Solid, One Broken Yellow Line

A two-lane road may be marked by one solid yellow line and one broken yellow line. In a situation like this, it is legal for the driver on the side with the broken yellow line to pass a slower vehicle. The driver must decide if it is safe to pass. When passing another vehicle, drivers must return to their lane before getting to a solid yellow line on their side of the road.

WATCH OUT !

You cannot cross a solid double yellow line to pass another vehicle. You also cannot pass when there is a broken yellow line with a solid yellow line on your side. Yet, it is OK to turn across a single or double yellow center line into a driveway.

▲ The driver to the right of the broken yellow line may pass.

Drive Smart!

Directions: Read each situation. If the last sentence of the situation is true, or correct, put an X in the TRUE box. If the last sentence is false, put an X in the FALSE box. Rewrite each false sentence to make it true.

1. You are driving on a two-lane road. The center line is marked with solid and broken yellow lines. The broken yellow line is on your side of the road. The law says you may pass a slower vehicle.

   TRUE ☐   FALSE ☐

   _____

   _____

   _____

2. You are driving on a two-lane road. The center line is marked with solid and broken yellow lines. The solid yellow line is on your side of the road. You may pass a slow truck.

   TRUE ☐   FALSE ☐

   _____

   _____

   _____

3. You are driving on a two-lane road. You would like to pass the slow van ahead of you. There are two solid yellow lines. The law says you may never cross double yellow center lines to pass another vehicle.

TRUE ☐   FALSE ☐

_____

_____

_____

4. You are on your way to the interstate. First, you must stop to get some gas for your vehicle. You may turn across a solid yellow center line to drive into a gas station.

TRUE ☐   FALSE ☐

_____

_____

_____

5. A driver moves over the center line to pass a slow vehicle. The driver can see solid and broken yellow center lines ahead. The solid yellow line is on the driver's side of the road. The driver may pass the slow vehicle even if it means crossing the solid yellow line before finishing the pass.

TRUE ☐   FALSE ☐

_____

_____

_____

CHAPTER 14: Special-Use Yellow Lane Lines

Before you read, you should know that:

▶ shared means a lane being used by more than one vehicle;

▶ reversible (re-VER-sih-bl) means being able to be used in an opposite way.

▶ oncoming traffic is traffic coming toward you.

After reading this chapter, you should be able to:

▶ tell how a **shared** left-turn lane is marked;

▶ tell how a **reversible** lane is marked;

▶ tell how to drive in a shared left turn lane;

▶ tell how to drive in a reversible lane.

PASS THAT TEST !

Shared Left-Turn Lane

A shared left-turn lane is a left-turn lane used by vehicles going in opposite directions. It is usually found in the center lane of the road. It is marked by a solid yellow line and a broken yellow line on each side of the center lane.

The center of the shared left-turn lane is marked with white left-turn arrows painted on the pavement. The white arrows show opposite left turns.

Drivers who want to turn left into a driveway must first enter the shared left-turn lane. The driver must cross a solid yellow line to enter the shared left-turn lane. The driver may turn left only from this lane. The driver may turn only when it is safe to turn.

When there is a lot of traffic, shared left-turn lanes also may be used to turn left into a street. Turn on your left-turn signal. Where traffic is clear, move into the shared left-turn lane and stop. When it is safe to drive, turn left.

▲ Shared left-turn lanes are used by vehicles making left turns.

WATCH OUT !

When using a shared left-turn lane, you must be very careful. Check for **oncoming** vehicles that want to use the same part of the lane. Do not drive a long way in a shared left-turn lane. Signal what you want to do, but only enter the lane when you are close to where you want to turn.

DID YOU KNOW?

Shared left-turn lanes often are used where there is a lot of traffic moving both ways. In most cases, many cars are turning left into driveways or shopping centers.

▲ Reversible lanes change directions during different times of the day.

PASS THAT TEST !

Reversible Lane

A reversible lane is a lane that changes direction during different times of the day. The lane is used by traffic going in one direction during one time of the day. The same lane is used by traffic going in the opposite direction during a different time of the day.

Reversible lanes help traffic to flow smoothly. Reversible lanes are marked with double yellow broken lines. Most of the time, signs on the side of the road tell drivers when the lanes are reversible.

Traffic lights above each lane also may be used to tell drivers which lanes they can use. The traffic lights tell drivers which lanes are to be used by drivers going in each direction.

Here is how reversible lane traffic lights work:

- A red X light over a lane tells the driver that the lane is closed. It is being used by oncoming traffic. Never drive in a lane marked by a red X.

- A yellow X over a lane warns drivers that the lane is going to be closed soon. The lane will soon have a red X over it. Drivers should move out of this lane as soon as possible.

- A flashing yellow X means that the lane is used only for left turns. These lanes should be used with caution (KAW-shun), or great care.

- A green arrow above a lane means that it is open to drivers facing the arrow.

▲ A red X over a lane tells the driver that the lane is closed.

▲ A yellow X over a lane warns drivers that the lane is going to be closed soon.

▼ A flashing yellow X means that the lane is used only for left turns.

▼ A green arrow above a lane means that it is open to drivers facing the arrow.

Drive Smart!

Directions: Read each sentence. Put an X in the box in front of the group of words that best finishes the sentence.

1. To turn left from a shared left-turn lane, you must

   ☐ first cross a solid yellow line on your side of the center line.

   ☐ first cross a solid white line.

   ☐ slow well in advance of the turn.

   ☐ first signal that you are moving right.

2. Cars moving in both directions

   ☐ never use the same lane.

   ☐ use the same shared left turn lane.

   ☐ must cross the lane markings at the same time.

   ☐ may not turn left at the same time.

3. You may use a shared left-turn lane

   ☐ when turning from a driveway into a road.

   ☐ only when turning right into a driveway.

   ☐ only in rural areas.

   ☐ when turning from a road into a driveway.

4. You are driving on a street with reversible lanes. The signal light above your lane is a flashing yellow X. You

   ☐ are in a lane for oncoming traffic.

   ☐ should move out of the lane.

   ☐ can keep going.

   ☐ are in a left-turn lane.

5. A red X over a reversible lane means the drivers in the lane

   ☐ may travel in the lane.

   ☐ are in a left-turn lane.

   ☐ must get out of the lane.

   ☐ are in a right-turn lane.

Section 5 Review   ROAD MARKINGS

Directions: These questions come from Chapters 12 -14. You may look back to these chapters if you need help in choosing the correct answer. Remember to read each sentence carefully. Then write X beside the answer you choose.

CHAPTER 12 White Road Markings

1. Broken white lane lines
    ___ a.   mark the right edge of the roadway.
    ___ b.   separate traffic moving in the same direction.
    ___ c.   separate traffic moving in opposite directions.
    ___ d.   mark pedestrian crosswalks.

2. Solid white lane lines
    ___ a.   separate traffic moving in opposite directions.
    ___ b.   mark the left edge of a roadway.
    ___ c.   warn drivers moving in the same direction that it is not safe to change lanes.
    ___ d.   warn drivers moving in opposite directions that it is not safe to pass.

3. You may only cross a broken white lane line
    ___ a.   when getting ready to make a left or right turn.
    ___ b.   when passing another vehicle.
    ___ c.   when it is safe to do so.
    ___ d.   only in an emergency.

4. The right lane of a street is marked with a white arrow to the right and the word only. Drivers in the right lane
    ___ a.   can go straight ahead or turn right.
    ___ b.   must turn right.
    ___ c.   must go straight.

5. As you drive a country road at night, you see a large "R", "X", "R" on the pavement. You are coming to
    ___ a.   a "T" intersection.   ___ b.   a sharp curve.
    ___ c.   a crossroad.   ___ d.   a railroad crossing.

CHAPTER 13 Yellow Road Markings

1. Yellow lane lines are used to
    ___ a.   mark the right edge of a roadway.
    ___ b.   mark pedestrian crosswalks.
    ___ c.   separate traffic moving in the same direction.
    ___ d.   separate traffic moving in opposite directions.

2. A broken yellow lane line tells drivers that
    ___ a.   they cannot pass.
    ___ b.   they may pass if it is safe to do so.
    ___ c.   they must turn left.
    ___ d.   they must turn right.

3. A double solid yellow lane line, or a single solid yellow lane line on your side of a center line means
    ___ a.   you may pass another vehicle if there is no traffic coming.
    ___ b.   you cannot cross the lane line for any reason.
    ___ c.   you may only cross the lane line to turn left into a driveway.
    ___ d.   the roadway gets narrow ahead.

4. A broken yellow lane line on your side of a solid yellow lane line means that
    ___ a.   you may pass another vehicle if it is safe to do so.
    ___ b.   you cannot pass another vehicle at this point.
    ___ c.   oncoming cars may pass.
    ___ d.   you are coming to an intersection.

CHAPTER 14 Special Use Yellow Lane Lines

1. To turn from a shared left turn lane, drivers must first
   ___ a. cross a solid yellow lane line on their side of the center line.
   ___ b. cross a solid white lane line.
   ___ c. slow well in advance of their turn.
   ___ d. first signal that they are going to move to the right.

2. Drivers traveling in opposite directions who want to use a shared left turn lane
   ___ a. never use the same shared left turn lane.
   ___ b. may not turn left at the same time.
   ___ c. use the same shared left turn lane.
   ___ d. must cross the lane markings at the same time.

3. Drivers may use a shared left turn lane
   ___ a. only on country roads.
   ___ b. when turning from or onto a driveway.
   ___ c. when turning at an intersection.
   ___ d. when making a "U" turn.

4. Reversible lanes can be identified by overhead signals, signs beside the road and
   ___ a. solid white lane lines.
   ___ b. double broken white lane lines.
   ___ c. solid yellow lane lines.
   ___ d. double broken yellow lane lines.

5. You are driving on a street marked with reversible lane markings. The signal light above the lane you are in is marked with a yellow "X." What should you do?
   ___ a. Move out of the lane. It will soon be used by oncoming traffic.
   ___ b. Move out of the lane. It is only open to oncoming traffic.
   ___ c. Stay in the lane. It is meant for traffic moving in the direction you are traveling.
   ___ d. Get ready to turn left. You are in a left turn lane.

SECTION 6: **SIGNS FOR LIFE**

Sections six and seven are about traffic control devices (dee-VYS-sez). Traffic control devices tell drivers where they are. They tell drivers how to get where they want to go. Some traffic control devices warn drivers of dangers ahead. Traffic control devices are an important part of driving.

You have already learned about pavement markings. Pavement markings are one kind of traffic control device. Traffic signs and signals are other kinds of traffic control devices. You will learn about traffic signs in section 7. Traffic signals are covered in section 8.

Signs, signals, and pavement markings tell you their meaning by their color and their shape. They also tell you their meaning by what they say and by pictures. Look for the different shapes, color, words, and pictures as you read each chapter.

Here are the colors used in all traffic control devices:

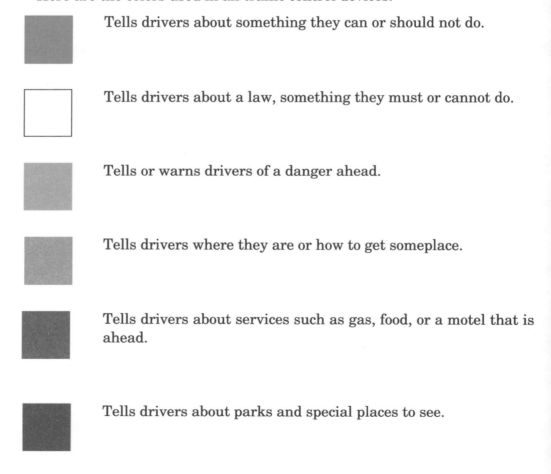

Tells drivers about something they can or should not do.

Tells drivers about a law, something they must or cannot do.

Tells or warns drivers of a danger ahead.

Tells drivers where they are or how to get someplace.

Tells drivers about services such as gas, food, or a motel that is ahead.

Tells drivers about parks and special places to see.

All traffic control devices used in the United States are based on the Manual of Uniform Traffic Control Devices. All states use this book as their guide when deciding on traffic signs, signals, and markings.

CHAPTER 15: Traffic Signs

Before you read, you should know that:

▶ **regulatory** means saying what can and cannot be done;

▶ to **exit** means to leave an area.

After reading this chapter, you should be able to:

▶ give five examples of **regulatory** signs;

▶ tell where five different red regulatory signs are used;

▶ tell where ten different white regulatory signs are used.

Traffic signs tell you about a law. They are regulatory signs. They tell you what you can or cannot do.

PASS THAT TEST !

Traffic signs with words on them are read from left to right and top to bottom. Traffic signs with arrows and other symbols (pictures) are read from bottom to top. They are usually red or white. Words on regulatory signs are black, red or white.

Drivers must watch for and obey all traffic signs. When this does not happen, there is a greater chance for a crash. This is why every driver must stay alert for the actions of other drivers.

Red Traffic Signs

▲ Stop Sign

A stop sign has eight sides. It is red with white letters. At a stop sign, you must stop. After you stop. you must check for cross traffic and pedestrians. You may drive on when it is safe.

▲ Yield Sign

A yield sign has three sides. It is red with white letters. When coming to a yield sign, you must slow your vehicle and be ready to stop. Check for cross traffic and pedestrians. If either is too close, you must stop and yield the right-of-way. You may go when it is safe.

▲ Do-not-enter Sign

A do-not-enter sign is round. It is red with white letters. Do-not-enter signs are found at the end of **exit** ramps, on one-way streets, and exit driveways.

▼ Railroad Crossbuck with red flashing lights

A railroad crossbuck is a white sign with black letters and an X. It is found at railroad crossings. You must stop if a train is near. If no train is coming, you may cross the tracks without stopping.

▼ Railroad Crossbuck with red flashing lights

Sometimes, you will see a crossbuck with red flashing lights.

▼ Railroad Crossbuck with red flashing lights and a crossing gate

At railroad crossings where there is a lot of traffic, the crossbuck may have both flashing red lights and a crossing gate. You must stop if the red lights are flashing and the gate is down.

White Regulatory Signs

Most white signs that regulate actions are higher than they are wide. They are read from top to bottom and from left to right.

▲ Daytime Speed Limit
Maximum speed during the day

▲ Nighttime Speed Maximum speed at night

▲ Truck Speed Limit Maximum truck speed at anytime

Signs that Direct Movement

▼ Left Turn Only
Drivers in this lane must turn left.

▼ One-Way Arrow
Traffic must move in the direction of the arrow.

Drivers coming to signs like these must steer around the objects in the direction the arrow points.

▼ Keep Right

▼ Keep Left

The People's Publishing Group, Inc.:*Studying for a Driver's License*

Signs that Restrict Movement

▲ No Parking
No one can park here from 8 A.M. to 4 P.M.

▲ No Bicycles
Bicycles are not allowed on this road.

▲ No Trucks
Trucks are not allowed to drive on this road.

CHECK YOUR STATE MANUAL Each state, city or local government has the right to post these signs where needed. State and local governments can decide on speed limits for roads, parking areas, bus stops, and other driving actions.

▲ No Right Turn
Drivers may not turn right at this street.

▲ No U Turn
Drivers are not allowed to make U-turns at this point or on this road.

▲ Handicapped Parking
Only vehicles with handicapped tags or a special permit may be parked in spaces marked with this picture.

Other Restrictions

◇ CENTER LANE
BUSES AND CAR POOLS ONLY
6 AM - 9 AM
MON - FRI

▲ HOV
High Occupancy (OK-yoo-pan-cee) Vehicle (HOV) lane; vehicles must have at least three or four passengers.

▼ Weight Limit
The maximum load allowed on a street, road, or bridge.

WALK ON LEFT FACING TRAFFIC

▲ Walking Facing Traffic
Pedestrians walking on this road must walk so they are facing traffic.

▼ No Parking Bus Stop
Parking space set aside for buses; other drivers cannot park here.

NO TRUCKS OVER 7000 LBS EMPTY WT

Drive Smart!

Directions: Look at the six signs. Then read each question. On the line, write the letter of the sign that answers each question.

▲ **A.** Crossbuck

▲ **B.** Yield

▲ **C.** Right Lane Must Turn Right

▲ **D.** Speed Limit

▲ **E.** Do Not Enter

▲ **F.** Keep Left

1. You are driving on a road and cannot remember the speed limit. Which sign tells you how fast you may go? _____

2. You want to turn left to get onto the entrance ramp to an interstate highway. The entrance and exit ramps are right beside each other. Which sign tells you which ramp not to take? _____

3. You are coming to an intersection. Which sign tells you who must give the right-of-way? _____

4. You are driving in the city. You are in the right lane of a four lane street. You want to go across an intersection. You are not sure it is a legal move. You look for something that will help before you get to the corner. Which sign tells you that drivers in your lane have to go right? _____

5. You are driving on a highway in a woods. You can hear a train. Yet, you do not see a train. Which sign tells you that you are close to a railroad crossing? _____

The People's Publishing Group, Inc.:*Studying for a Driver's License*

CHAPTER 16: Caution Signs

Before you read, you should know that:

- a **median** (MEE-dee-an) is a center paved area that runs between lanes of traffic traveling in opposite directions;

- a **curve** (kurv) is a bend in the road;

- a **construction zone** is a place where road work is taking place;

- **FT** means foot or feet (12 inches equals 1 foot).

- to **detour** (DE-toor) is to leave the road you want to drive on because the road you want to use is closed;

- a **school zone** is an area around a school;

After reading this chapter, you will be able to:

- know how to read yellow caution signs;

- know how to read orange caution signs;

- give three examples of special caution signs.

PASS THAT TEST !

Most caution signs are yellow with black letters. They are shaped like a diamond. Caution signs also are called warning signs.

Caution signs tell you about the kind of road ahead. They tell you about the condition of the road. They also tell you about things that could make driving more of a danger. Often, the warning is shown as a picture.

Signs that Warn of Changes in Traffic Movement

▼ Two-Way Traffic

This sign tells drivers that the road they are on will change from one-way to two-way traffic.

▼ Center Barrier

This sign tells drivers that there is an object in the road ahead; they will need to steer around the object.

▼ Divided Highway Ahead

This sign tells drivers that the two-way road they are on is going to change to a highway with a center **median.**

▼ End Divided Highway

This sign tells drivers that the divided highway they are on is going to become a road with a center line.

Signs That Warn of Changes in Road Conditions

▲ Pavement Ends
This sign tells drivers that the hard surface road is going to end.

▲ Bump
This sign tells drivers to slow down. There is a bump in the road ahead.

▲ Dip
This sign tells drivers to slow down. There is a dip, or low spot, in the road ahead.

▲ Soft Shoulder
This sign warns drivers that the shoulder (SHOHL-der), or edge of the road, is soft. Drivers should watch for this danger ahead.

▲ Icy Road
This sign warns drivers that the road is slippery ahead.

▲ Steep Incline
This sign warns there is a steep hill ahead.

Signs That Warn of Changes in Road Width

▼ Merge Left

This sign tells drivers that the right lane ends ahead. Drivers in the right lane must merge to the left.

▼ Added Lane

This sign tells drivers that a road merges from the right. The merge lane is long. Drivers entering from the right do not have to enter the right travel lane quickly.

▼ Road Narrows

This sign tells drivers that the pavement ahead is not as wide as it is where they are driving now. They should be careful when meeting other vehicles.

▼ Narrow Bridge

This sign tells drivers that the bridge ahead is not very wide. Drivers should slow down and be careful if they meet an oncoming vehicle on the bridge.

The People's Publishing Group, Inc.:*Studying for a Driver's License*

Signs That Warn of Changes in the Direction of the Road

Curve signs are read from the bottom up to the top.

▼ Curve (under 30 mph)

This sign warns drivers of a sharp, 90-degree **curve.** It means slow to the speed you see on the sign. The curve is very sharp.

▼ Curve (over 30 mph)

This sign warns drivers of a curve less than 90 degrees. While, the danger may be less than on a sharper turn, there still is a danger. Drivers should slow to the speed on the sign.

▼ Reverse Turn

This sign is sometimes is called an "S" curve sign. It warns drivers that they will be driving through two sharp turns close together.

▼ Winding Road

This sign warns drivers of a winding road. The road makes many turns, one after another. Drivers need to be alert for on-coming vehicles.

Signs That Warn of Intersections Ahead

▼ Crossroad

This sign warns drivers that another road crosses the road they are traveling on.

▼ Side Road

This sign warns drivers that another road intersects (in-ter-SEKS), or meets, the road they are on. The roads do not cross each other.

▼ T Intersection

This sign warns drivers that the road they are on ends when it intersects with another road ahead. The driver will have to turn left or right.

▼ Y Intersection

This sign warns drivers that the road they are on splits into two roads going left and right. They should be alert for cars cutting across their lane at the corner.

Signs That Warn of Something Crossing the Road

These signs use pictures. They warn you that what the sign shows is in the area and crosses the road often. Drivers should be alert and ready to stop.

▼ Bicycle

▼ Pedestrians

▼ Deer

▼ Cattle

▼ Tractor

Signs That Warn of Special Problems in Construction Zones

⚡ **Construction zone** signs are orange. They use black letters to tell drivers of dangers ahead. The signs are read from the top to the bottom. Sometimes, pictures are used instead of letters.

▼ Blasting Zone (1)   ▼ Blasting Zone (2)   ▼ Blasting Zone (3)

A blasting zone area warning is made up of three signs:
   (1) Blasting Zone 1000 FT   (2) Turn Off 2-Way Radio   (3) End Blasting Zone
Drivers must turn off two-way radios to prevent an explosion (eks-PLO-shun).

▼ Drop Off

This sign warns drivers that the road is getting a new, hard surface. As a result, one lane is 2 to 4 inches lower than the next lane. Be careful. You can easily lose control of your car if you change lanes.

▼ Advanced Flagger Sign

This sign tells drivers that a highway worker is controlling traffic ahead. Be ready to stop. Roadwork machines or workers may suddenly move onto the road.

▼ Detour

This sign warns drivers that the road they are on is closed ahead. They should follow the **detour** signs to get back to the road they were first driving on.

⚡ Some warning signs are not diamond shaped. Their shape tells drivers of special dangers. Watch for these warning signs when you are driving a vehicle.

▼ Chevron Alignment

This sign is used with curve signs. It is placed beside the road on the curve. It warns drivers that the curve is sharp and a danger. SLOW DOWN

▼ No Passing Zone

This sign is used with solid yellow center lines. It is placed on the left side of the road so drivers can easily see it.

▼ Object Markers

These signs tell drivers about things close to the roadway. The angle of the lines point down in the direction drivers should pass the object.

▼ Slow-Moving Vehicle

This sign is used to warn drivers that the vehicle ahead moves at a slow speed. It is most often seen on farm tractors, horse-drawn vehicles, and construction equipment (ee-KWIP-ment).

The People's Publishing Group, Inc.:*Studying for a Driver's License*

▼ School Zone

This sign warns drivers that they are coming to a **school zone.** During school hours, drivers should slow to the school zone speed limit. They should be alert for children on their way to or from school.

▼ School Crossing

This sign warns drivers that they are coming to a school crossing. Drivers should be alert for children crossing the street.

▼ Railroad Warning

This sign tells drivers that there is a railroad crossing ahead. Drivers should be alert for a train coming. Drivers should also check ahead for flashing red lights and crossing gates.

Drive Smart!

Directions: Look at each sign. Then read each question. On the line, write the letter of the sign that answers the first question. Read the second question. Write your answer in a complete sentence.

▲ **A.** Flagger

▲ **B.** Two-Way Traffic

▲ **C.** School Zone

▲ **D.** Chevron

▲ **E.** Narrow Bridge

▲ **F.** Deer

▲ **G.** Added Lane

▲ **H.** Divided Highway Ahead

1. You are driving on a divided roadway. Which sign tells you that the road you are on is going to change to a road with a center line? _____
    What should you do?

    _____

    _____

2. You are driving on a two-lane road. Which sign tells you that there is a narrow bridge ahead? _____
What should you do?

_____

_____

3. You are driving on a four-lane road. Which sign tells you that traffic may merge from the right? _____   What should you do?

_____

_____

4. It is 8 A.M. on a Monday in the month of March. You are driving on a street in a city. Which sign tells you that you are coming to a school zone? _____
What should you do?

_____

_____

5. You are driving on a two lane road in the country. Which sign tells you that the curve ahead is very sharp? _____   What should you do?

_____

_____

6. You are driving on a country road. Which sign warns you that something may be crossing the road ahead? _____
What should you do?

_____

_____

7. You are driving on a two-lane road in a construction zone. Which sign tells you that you may have to stop? _____   What should you do?

_____

_____

CHAPTER 17: Signs that Guide You

Before you read, you should know that:

- ▶ recreation (rek-ree-AY-shun) is something people do to relax and enjoy themselves.

- ▶ a route (rout) is a road that can be traveled on;

- ▶ guide (gyd) means to show you the way to something;

- ▶ a junction (JUNK-shun) is where two roads meet;

- ▶ interstate (IN-ter-stayt) is a road that often crosses over two or more states;

After reading this chapter, you should be able to:

- ▶ read four signs that help you get where you want to go;

- ▶ read ten **recreation** or roadside service signs;

- ▶ read six **route** marker signs.

Guide signs that give directions are green. Guide signs that tell about travel and emergency services are blue. Guide signs that tell about parks and places to see are brown.

Guide Signs That Give Direction and Tell Distance

These signs tell drivers where they are. They also tell drivers how to get somewhere. They tell drivers how far away a place is.

▲ Exits
Exit signs tell drivers where an exit goes. Exit signs tell drivers the number of an exit, where it goes, and how far ahead it is.

▼ Direction
Direction signs tell drivers which way to go to get somewhere.

▲ **Junction**
Junction signs tell drivers the name and/or number of roads that cross or intersect other roads.

▲ Distance
Distance signs tell drivers how far it is to towns, cities, and major roadways.

Recreation and Areas of Interest (IN-ter-est)

These signs tell drivers about places they can go for recreation. They also tell drivers about places that are interesting to visit. The kinds of things people can see or do are shown on the signs. The signs shown here are just a few of the signs you may see along a highway.

▲ Lighthouse

▲ Ranger Station

▲ Canoeing

▲ Swimming

▲ Skating

▲ Trail

Roadside Services

These signs tell drivers about services they may need. The signs say that the services are nearby. Watch for these signs beside the road. On interstate highways, you will often see services listed on signs as you get near an interchange. The signs shown here are just a few of the signs you may see along a highway.

▲ Rest Area

▲ Fuel

▲ Police

▲ Hospital

The People's Publishing Group, Inc.:*Studying for a Driver's License*

▲ First Aid

▲ Food

▲ Camping

DID YOU KNOW?

Interstate routes are marked with one or two numbers. Interstate highways marked with odd numbers (5 to 95) run north and south. Interstate highways marked with even numbers (4 to 94) run east and west.

Sometimes, interstate, U.S., and state routes have signs that say **Business Loop** or **Bypass.** This means that a road with the same number goes into or around the city.

When an interstate route has a loop that goes across a city, the route is given three numbers. The first number is even (2, 4, 6, or 8). For example, I-95 becomes I-495. This also is true if a loop connects one interstate to another interstate highway.

When a section of interstate goes into a city but does not come out, it also is given three numbers. The first number is an odd number (3, 5, 7, or 9). For example, I-95 becomes I-395.

Route Markers

These signs tell drivers the route number and the kind of road they are on. Route signs often use different shapes and colors. The different colors and shapes tell you that the road is a town, county, state, U.S., or **interstate** highway.

▲ Interstate

▲ U.S. Route

▲ State Route

▲ County Route

▲ Milepost

Drive Smart!

Directions: Read each situation. Put an X in the box in front of the words that best finish the situation sentence.

1. You are driving south on Interstate 95 (I-95). As you near a city, you see a sign that says EXIT I-395 Baltimore. This tells you that I-395

   ☐ goes around the city of Baltimore.

   ☐ goes across the city of Baltimore.

   ☐ goes into the city of Baltimore and stops.

   ☐ goes to a different city.

DID YOU KNOW?

Mileposts are numbered from the south and west borders of a state. For example, milepost one (1) is 1 mile from the south or west side of a state.

All roads do not start at a border. For these roads, the numbers start at the road's south or west junction.

Mileposts serve as guides to drivers. In case of a crash, they also help tell exactly where the crash can be found.

2. An exit sign tells drivers how far it is

☐ to the nearest gas station.

☐ to the nearest rest area.

☐ to the next city or town.

☐ to the nearest place to get food.

Directions: Now look at the signs. Read the situation. Then write the letter of the sign that shows what you are looking for.

▲ **A.** Swimming   ▲ **B.** Fuel   ▲ **C.** Food

▲ **D.** Lighthouse   ▲ **E.** First Aid

You are driving on an interstate highway.

3. You are hungry and are looking for a place to eat. _____

4. You would like to see a lighthouse that you think is near where you are driving. _____

5. You look at your gas gauge (gayj) and see that you need gas. _____

6. It is a hot day and a cool swim would be a good thing to do. _____

The People's Publishing Group, Inc.:*Studying for a Driver's License*

Section 6 Review   SIGNS FOR LIFE

Directions: These questions come from Chapters 15 -17. You may look back to these chapters if you need help in choosing the correct answer. Remember to read each sentence carefully. Then write X beside the answer you choose.

CHAPTER 15 Traffic Signs

1. Regulatory signs
   ___   a.   warn drivers of dangers ahead.
   ___   b.   give distances to points ahead.
   ___   c.   identify the road you are on.
   ___   d.   tell drivers what they can and cannot do.

2. Regulatory signs are generally red or black on a white background and may be
   ___   a.   round, square, pennant or diamond shaped
   ___   b.   eight sided, rectangle, triangle or "X" shaped.
   ___   c.   diamond, pennant, eight sided or square shaped.
   ___   d.   diamond, pennant, eight sided or "X" shaped.

3. Which of the following is a regulatory sign?
   ___   a.   Diamond sign = Narrow bridge
   ___   b.   Pennant sign = end no passing zone
   ___   c.   Triangle = Yield Right-Of-Way
   ___   d.   Rectangle = Troy — 35 miles

▲ 1

▲ 2

▲ 3

4. The sign shown in number 1 above means that drivers
   ___   a.   must stop only if there is cross traffic.
   ___   b.   must slow and yield right-of-way to pedestrians.
   ___   c.   must come to a stop and go only when it is safe to go.
   ___   d.   may turn right without stopping.

5. The sign shown in number 2 above means that drivers
   ___   a.   must slow and yield right-of-way before turning.
   ___   b.   cannot turn left.
   ___   c.   cannot turn right.
   ___   d.   must stop and then go when it is safe.

6. The sign shown in number 3 above means that drivers
   ___   a.   should cross the tracks as quickly as possible.
   ___   b.   must come to a full stop at the railroad crossing.
   ___   c.   must check for trains and stop if there is a train coming.
   ___   d.   should not cross the tracks until directed by a train crew person.

▲ 1   ▲ 2   ▲ 3   ▲ 4

1. The sign shown in number 1 above tells drivers that
   ___ a. the road ends ahead.
   ___ b. there is an intersection ahead.
   ___ c. the road is slippery.
   ___ d. the road curves sharply.

2. The sign shown in number 2 above tells drivers that
   ___ a. because of uneven road surfaces they may lose control if they change lanes.
   ___ b. they should watch for vehicles on the shoulder of the road.
   ___ c. they should watch out for highway workers.
   ___ d. there is loose gravel on the road ahead.

3. The sign shown in number 3 above tells drivers that
   ___ a. they should change lanes to allow drivers to merge with traffic.
   ___ b. they should slow to allow drivers to merge with traffic.
   ___ c. merging traffic has a long merge lane and time to adjust speed and position.
   ___ d. merging traffic must stop before entering the major traffic lane.

4. The sign shown in number 4 above means that drivers
   ___ a. must come to a stop for the school crossing.
   ___ b. must slow and be ready to stop for school buses.
   ___ c. must not exceed 15 miles per hour in a school zone.
   ___ d. warns drivers that they are coming to a school zone.

CHAPTER 17 Signs that Guide You

1. Guide signs are what colors?
   ___ a. Red, yellow, and green   ___ b Green yellow, and blue
   ___ c. Brown, yellow, and green   ___ d. Brown, blue, and green

2. Guide signs tell drivers
   ___ a. about laws that control what they can or cannot do.
   ___ b. about dangers on the road ahead.
   ___ c. points of interest, where they are and services available.
   ___ d. when it is safe to pass.

3. Mile markers on Interstate highways are numbered from
   ___ a. east to west and south to north.
   ___ b. west to east and north to south.
   ___ c. west to east and south to north.
   ___ d. east to west and north to south.

4. A driver is traveling north toward Washington DC. on I-95. As he gets near the city a sign over the roadway says I-395 to Washington, D.C. This means that I-395
   ___ a. goes around Washington, D.C.
   ___ b. goes through Washington, D.C.
   ___ c. goes into Washington, D.C. and ends there.
   ___ d. goes to a different city.

5. Direction signs tell drivers
   ___ a. the number of state roadways.
   ___ b. information about gas and food.
   ___ c. the distance to various cities.
   ___ d. which way to go to get someplace.

SECTION 7: LIGHTS FOR LIFE

CHAPTER 18: Traffic Signal Lights

Before you read, you should know that:
▶ a **signal** (SĬG-nal) is something that directs you;
▶ a **lens** (lenz) is the covering of a signal light;
▶ a **billboard** (BIL-bord) is a large sign with a message about the road or traffic;
▶ a **message sign** uses lights to tell drivers about road conditions.

After reading this chapter, you should be able to:
▶ give four examples of where traffic **signal** lights may be used;
▶ give three examples of times when flashing red lights may be used;
▶ tell what you do when coming upon a flashing red light;
▶ tell what you do when coming upon a flashing yellow light.

Traffic signal lights tell drivers things they must know to drive safely. Traffic signal lights tell drivers what the law says they may do. They also tell drivers what they cannot do. Some traffic lights warn drivers of dangers ahead.

Some traffic signal lights are not well known. For this reason, their message is not well understood. To be a safe driver, you need to know about all traffic signal lights.

PASS THAT TEST !

Traffic Control Signal Lights

Most traffic control signal lights are meant to be read from top to bottom. Some traffic control signal lights are meant to be read from left to right. The top or left light is red. The middle light is yellow. The bottom or right light is green.

Traffic control signal lights tell which driver has the right-of-way. A green light means the driver facing the light may go after making sure the way is clear of pedestrians and vehicles.

A yellow light means that the light is about to turn red. A yellow light is not a signal to the driver to drive faster. Drivers coming to a yellow light should slow down and be ready to stop.

A red light means that drivers must stop.

▲ Traffic Control Signal Light

▼ Traffic Control Signal Light

▲ Green Signal
Light and Red
Arrow

▲ Red Signal Light
and Green Arrow

▲ Green Traffic
Signal Light and
Green Arrow

▲ Traffic Signal
Lights and Arrow
Lenses

▼ Traffic Signal
Lights and Arrow
Lenses

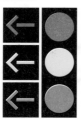

WATCH OUT !

A driver may enter an intersection on a red light only when making a "Right or Left Turn on Red." To make a turn on red, drivers must first do these things:

• Check to see if there is a left or right green arrow with the red traffic light. If there is a green arrow, and it is safe to drive, a driver may turn without stopping.

• Check to see if there is a **No Turn On Red** light. If there is such a sign, drivers must stop. They may not make a turn. If there is no such sign, drivers must stop and check for cross traffic and pedestrians. When it is safe, drivers may turn.

PASS THAT TEST !

Arrow Signal Lights

Red, yellow, and green arrows are sometimes used with traffic signals at intersections. The red arrow is at the top, the yellow in the middle, and the green arrow on the bottom.

Sometimes, a red arrow is used with a green signal light. The red arrow means drivers cannot turn even when the traffic signal is green.

Sometimes, a green arrow is used with a red signal light. The green arrow means that drivers may turn right (or left) without stopping. The turn must be free of traffic.

Sometimes, a green arrow is used with a green traffic signal light. The green arrow tells drivers that they may turn left. The oncoming traffic has a red light. This kind of signal may be used at the start or end of a light change.

Sometimes, you may make left turns even after a green arrow goes off. You may turn if there is no red arrow. The signal light is must be green. A sign may warn drivers that turning traffic must yield the right-of-way.

Sometimes there are two sets of traffic signal lights next to each other. One set of lights has round red, yellow, and green **lenses** (LEN-zez).

The other set of lights has red, yellow, and green arrow lenses. The arrow signals are used to tell drivers turning left or right that they:

• may turn ahead of oncoming traffic;

• must wait to turn until oncoming traffic has stopped.

Flashing Signal Lights

Flashing signal lights are red or yellow. They are used in places where there is a greater chance for a crash. They can be found at intersections, pedestrian crossings, and school crossings. They also can be found in road construction zones.

PASS THAT TEST !

Flashing Red Lights

Flashing red lights mean **STOP.** They are used to tell drivers that they are coming to an intersection where there is a greater danger of a crash. Drivers must stop their vehicles at the intersection.

Drivers must always stop at a flashing red signal light. After stopping, drivers must check for vehicles and pedestrians. They may drive on when it is safe.

PASS THAT TEST !

Flashing Yellow Lights

Flashing yellow lights are used to warn drivers to be alert. There is a driving situation ahead that is not safe. (For example, flashing yellow lights are used at intersections. They also are used to warn drivers of a school-crossing zone.) You should slow down for a flashing yellow light. Be ready to stop to keep from getting into a crash.

Flashing yellow lights also are used in road repair and construction zones. Flashing lights may be used on a **billboard** to spell out a special message. The **message sign** may tell drivers that there is a construction zone or special danger ahead.

Flashing yellow arrow tells drivers to change lanes left or right.

A special flashing light board is used to tell drivers that the road shoulder ahead is closed for repair. The lights may flash in one of two ways:

- four lights set in a straight line;
- four lights set in the shape of a box.

DID YOU KNOW?

Arrow signal lights are used most often in large cities. They also are used on highways where many vehicles make turns. Arrow signals let more vehicles make turns. They also reduce the danger of turning vehicles being in crashes with oncoming vehicles.

▲ Flashing Red Light

DID YOU KNOW?

At times, only a few vehicles use an intersection during the night hours. When this happens, traffic signal lights may be changed to flashing red. The light may flash red for vehicles on only one road. Sometimes, the lights may flash red on both roads.

▲ Flashing Yellow Light

▼ Flashing yellow arrow tells drivers to turn left.

▼ Flashing yellow arrow tells drivers to turn right.

▼ Four flashing lights tell the road is closed for repair.

▼ Four flashing lights tell the road is closed for repair.

Pedestrian Signals

Pedestrian signal lights may use words or picture messages. The words or pictures may be white or orange.

The word **WALK** means that it is legal for pedestrians to cross the street. A picture of a pedestrian walking also means it is legal to cross the street. This is like a green traffic signal light. Pedestrians should check for traffic before starting to cross.

When the words **DON'T WALK** start to flash, the walk signal is going to end. A picture of a hand raised in a stop position also means the walk signal is going to end. This is like a yellow traffic signal light. Pedestrians in the street may keep walking across. No pedestrian should start to cross the street.

When the words **DON'T WALK** stop flashing but remain steady, no pedestrian should enter the street. No pedestrian should enter the street if the raised hand stops flashing but remains steady. This is like a red traffic signal light. Pedestrians crossing against a steady **DON'T WALK** can be given a ticket for not obeying a traffic signal.

▲ Walk Sign

▲ Pedestrian Sign

▲ Don't Walk Sign

▼ Don't Walk Sign

▲ Hand Sign

▼ Hand Sign

Drive Smart!

Directions: Read each situation. Write an answer to the question. Give at least one reason for why you believe as you do. A driving law must be part of your answer.

1. You want to make a right turn at the next corner. The signal light is green. A right-turn arrow below the green light is red. Is it OK to make a right turn? Why or why not?

   _____

   _____

2. Traffic is moving at 25 mph. Just before you get to the pedestrian crosswalk lines, a traffic signal light turns from green to yellow. Could you get a ticket for not stopping? Why or why not?

   _____

   _____

3. It is 11:30 P.M. You are driving home. You don't see any other vehicles. You come to an intersection with a flashing red light. Must you stop? Why or why not?

   _____

   _____

4. At the next intersection you see a flashing yellow light. Must you stop? Why or why not?

   _____

   _____

5. You are going to walk across the street. Just as you get to the corner, the DON'T WALK signal starts to flash. The people next to you start to cross the street. Should you also cross? Why or why not?

   _____

   _____

Hints to Help You Pass that Test!

Short Answer

Short answer questions test how well you remember facts. The only way to answer these questions correctly is to know your facts.

When rereading short answer questions, watch to see if your need to write only a few words, or if you need to write a complete sentence. This can make the difference between having your answer marked right or wrong. Here are some hints on how to do well on short answer test questions.

Hint # 1

Watch for how the questions is written. Are you being asked, "how", "why", "when", or "where"?

Directions: Write a sentence to answer each question.

1. How do you make a left turn onto a one-way street?
2. Why should drivers yield the right-of-way to the vehicle on the right at a four-way intersection?
3. When must traffic always turn right?
4. Where will you find a chevron alignment?

Hint # 2

Answer just the question. Do not spend time writing long answers with lots of words. This leaves you time for the rest of the test. If you have time, go back and check your answers.

Directions: Tell how to turn your wheels when parking downhill.

Right: When parking downhill, you should turn your wheels toward the curb.

Too many words: First carefully steer your vehicle within 12 inches of the curb. You may have to pull forward and backward to do this. Then turn your wheels toward the curb by gently guiding the steering wheel. Place your vehicle in park. Turn off the engine. Put on your paring brake.

Hint # 3

If you are not sure of the answer, try to write something anyway. You may know more than you think you know. At least try writing a general answer to the question. Your answer may be counted partly right.

What should you do when you see a road construction sign?

General answer: You should look for road work ahead.

(What else could have been said to make a better answer?)

The People's Publishing Group, Inc.:*Studying for a Driver's License*

Section 7 Review   LIGHTS FOR LIFE

Directions: These questions come from Chapter 18. You may look back to this chapter if you need help in choosing the correct answer. Remember to read each sentence carefully. Then write X beside the answer you choose.

CHAPTER 18 Traffic Signal Lights

1. A steady red signal light or steady red arrow with a no-right-turn-on-red sign, tells drivers
   ___ a.   they must stop and wait for a green light or arrow.
   ___ b.   they must stop and proceed, or drive on, with caution.
   ___ c.   turn right.
   ___ d.   turn right when the road is free of traffic.

2. A driver wants to make a right turn at an intersection. The traffic signal light is red, but an arrow below the light is green. The driver should
   ___ a.   stop and then turn right.
   ___ b.   stop and wait for the light to change green.
   ___ c.   turn right; he has the right-of-way.
   ___ d.   turn right, but yield-right-of-way to pedestrians.

3. A flashing Don't Walk signal means that
   ___ a.   pedestrians should not start across the street.
   ___ b.   the light has just come on.
   ___ c.   pedestrians should yield-right-of-way to drivers.
   ___ d.   drivers can start through the intersection.

4. A driver is close to a traffic signal light when it changes from green to yellow. The driver should
   ___ a.   brake hard and stop.
   ___ b.   speed up to get through the intersection.
   ___ c.   stop and then drive through the intersection.
   ___ d.   check traffic and be ready to stop if the light turns red.

5. A driver in a construction zone sees a flashing light sign with four (4) lights in a row. There is no lighted arrow ahead. This should tell drivers that
   ___ a.   some of the bulbs are burned out.
   ___ b.   they should change lanes to the left.
   ___ c.   they should change lanes to the right.
   ___ d.   the shoulder ahead is closed for repair.

CHAPTER 19: Serious Traffic Offenses

Before you read, you should know that:

▶ to **suspend** (sus-PEND) means to take away a right for a length of time (for example, John's dad suspended his right to drive for a week);

▶ to **revoke** (ree-VOHK) means to take away someone's license (the judge decided to revoke her license);

▶ a **traffic offense** (uh-FENS) is doing something that is against a traffic law;

▶ a **suspension** (sus-PEN-shun) is the taking away of a driver's license for a certain amount of time. This could be 30, 60, 90, or 180 days;

▶ a **revocation** (reh-voh-KAY-shun) is the process of taking away a person's privilege (PRIH-vih-lej) to drive. The court or state sets a length of time the driver must wait before applying for a new drivers license. The new license often costs extra;

After reading this chapter, you should be able to:

▶ tell what a serious driving offense is;

▶ give four examples of serious driving offenses;

▶ give three examples of what may happen when a person commits a serious driving offense.

CHECK YOUR STATE MANUAL

Each state has the right to **suspend** or **revoke** the license of a driver who has committed a serious traffic offense. Each state has its own set of rules to deal with drivers with first and repeat traffic offenses.

Here are some other traffic offenses covered by state law:
• having a record of many vehicle crashes;
• not being able to drive safely;
• using a driver's license that is not legal;
• not showing up in court when told to do so after committing a traffic offense;
• using a car to run away from a police officer;
• not paying a fine or fines for a traffic offense.

▼ Anyone who commits a serious traffic offense may go to court.

PASS THAT TEST !

Traffic Offenses

There are some **traffic offenses** that are very harmful to yourself. They also can be very harmful to others. People who are caught committing these traffic offenses are arrested (ah-RES-ted). They may be taken to jail.

Anyone who commits a serious traffic offense must go to court. A driver who has committed a traffic offense will likely receive a penalty (PEN-ul-tee). The penalty may be a fine. A fine means the driver will have to pay some amount of money.

The penalty also may mean the driver being sent to a school for people who commit traffic offenses. A fee is charged to go to the school.

When a driver breaks a traffic law the first time, the driver is treated as a first offender (uh-FEN-der). For a first offense, drivers pay a fine. They may be sent to a traffic safety school.

If the driver breaks the same law a second or third time, the driver is called a **repeat offender.** The penalties for repeat offenses often are more harsh. There may be a **suspension** or **revocation** of the driver's license. This is often true for persons who commit serious traffic offenses.

Reckless Driving

Reckless driving occurs when a person drives without concern for the safety of other persons. In reckless driving, the driver knows that the driving is not being done in a safe way. Yet, the driver chooses to drive that way.

Penalties for reckless driving can be from $25 to $500. The driver may spend from five to ninety days in jail.

Racing on the Highway

No driver may race another driver on a highway. The penalty for a first offense can be a fine of up to $200. The penalty for a second offense in one year can be a fine of up to $300. The penalty for a third offense can be a fine of up to $500. The driver also might have to stay in jail for six months.

Alcohol

Every state has a law making 21 the minimum age to drink anything with alcohol (AL-ko-hall) in them. Such drinks as beer and wine have alcohol in them. Alcohol can confuse a person's thinking. Alcohol affects each person in a different way. For this reason, people who drive should not drink anything with alcohol in it. The best advice is: "If you drink, never drive."

Every state has an Implied Consent Law. This law says that any driver stopped by a police officer must take a blood alcohol content (BAC) test when asked to do so. This test finds out how much alcohol there is in the driver's blood. The police officer must believe the driver has been drinking alcohol to ask for this test.

▲ Any driver stopped by a police officer must take a BAC test.

Every state has an Implied Consent Law. This law says that you are required to take a test for alchohol if stopped by the police. Drivers who refuse to take a BAC test will have their licenses suspended.

▲ Illegal Drugs make a person a very unsafe driver.

Other Drugs

Besides alcohol, other drugs you take can make you an unsafe driver. Some drugs given to you by a doctor for an illness you have can make it unsafe for you to drive. Even some drugs you can buy at the store, such as cough medicine, can make it unsafe for you to drive. Sometimes, two drugs taken together can seriously reduce your ability to drive safely or to drive at all.

Illegal drugs, or drugs bought on the street that are not supposed to be sold, can make a person a very unsafe driver.

Ask a doctor about how a drug will affect your driving before you take the drug and drive. Read the labels of drugs you buy at the store. Do not drive if it says the drug will make you sleepy.

▲ Read the labels of drugs you buy at the store.

WATCH OUT !

A driver who has used alcohol or other drugs while driving may be sent to a clinic. The cost for such a clinic can be several hundred dollars. The driver may be sent to jail for some length of time. The driver may have to pay a fine of several hundred dollars.

DID YOU KNOW?

The total cost for being convicted of DWI could be about $7,000 or more. Lawyer's fees, extra insurance cost for three years, a fine, loss of work while in jail, and other costs are all part of this $7,000. Plus, the extra cost to a driver as the result of suspension or revocation of a drivers license is not part of the $7,000 cost.

Studies show that nearly half of all traffic deaths result from drinking and then driving. The record for young drivers (those 16 to 19) is often worse.

Drive Smart!

Directions: Read the sentence or statement. Fill in the blank with the correct answer.

1. In the state in which you live, a driver will be charged with the traffic offense of DUI/DWI if their BAC is higher than _____.

2. Three serious traffic offenses for which a driver may be sent to jail are _____, _____, and _____.

3. Alcohol is part of about _____ percent of all traffic crash deaths.

4. Besides alcohol, three other drugs that could affect your ability to drive are
_____, _____, and
_____.

5. You have been stopped by a police officer who thinks you have been drinking. The officer asks you to take a breath test for BAC. You refuse. The officer has the right to _____.

6. A police officer stops and arrests a driver on a charge of reckless driving. The driver is convicted of the traffic offense of reckless driving. Most likely, the driver will _____.

CHECK YOUR STATE MANUAL

Every state has set a limit on the amount of alcohol a person can drink and still drive. This is called Blood Alochol Concentration (**BAC**). A BAC of 0.08 percent or 0.10 percent is enough for the driver to be convicted or a charge of "driving under the influence" (IN-floo-ens) or DUI. The charge could be called "driving while intoxicated" (in-TOKS-ih-kay-ted) or DWI.

A 0.08 percent to 0.10 percent BAC is equal to four or five shots of liquor, bottles of beer, or glasses of wine.

Nearly half of the states have laws that make it illegal to have an open container (bottle or can) of alcohol in hte passenger area of a car or truck. Many states have laws about alcohol for drivers under 21 years of age. In some states, drivers between the ages of 16 and 21 may lose their license to drive if their BAC is over 0.02 percent.

In a few states, drivers 16 to 19 years of age may lose their driver's license if their BAC is anything over 0.00 percent These laws, sometimes called **BOOZE and LOSE,** are the result of the high crash and death rates of young drivers who have been drinking.

For 16-19 year olds, after four drinks, the chance of being killed in a crash is 40 times greater than for no drinking and driving. By six drinks, the risk of a fatal crash is 90 times higher than the risk for an older person.

CHAPTER 20: Special Traffic Safety Laws

Before you read, you should know that:

▶ a passenger (PAS-en-jer) is anyone who rides in a vehicle;

▶ a safety restraint (ree-STRAYNT) is a belt that holds a person on the seat of the vehicle;

▶ an air bag is a special bag that inflates or blows up to protect a person during a crash;

▶ a funeral (FYOO-ner-al) procession (pro-SEH-shun) is a number of vehicles driving is a line to honor a person who has died.

After reading this chapter, you should be able to:

▶ give three examples of special traffic safety laws;

▶ tell how these three laws make for safer driving.

DID YOU KNOW?

People should wear safety belts even when their vehicle has one or more air bags.

About 70 percent of all persons killed when riding in a vehicle are drivers. Injuries to the head, throat, and/or chest cause about 70 percent of these deaths.

One of the purposes of an air bag is to prevent these kinds of injuries. The best protection (pro-TEK-shun) in a crash is given if you have both safety restraints and an **air bag.**

PASS THAT TEST !

Safety Restraints

Nearly all states have a law that says a driver and front-seat **passenger** must use **safety restraints.** Some states have laws that say passengers up to 12 or 16 years of age must use safety restraints anytime they ride in a vehicle.

All states say any child under the age of 4 must be in a child-restraint seat. This safety seat must meet the standards or rules of the United States Department of Transportation.

If a child is under 6 years of age but is at least 4, the child must wear a safety belt. The child also may be in a child-restraint seat.

▼ Air bags do not take the place of seat belts.

PASS THAT TEST !

Funeral Processions

Drivers in a **funeral** procession should drive at a close, but safe, distance from each other. Drivers in a funeral procession should drive to the right side of the road.

No one may drive between the cars of a funeral procession. Vehicles in a funeral procession may have special flags. They may be driving with their headlights on.

The People's Publishing Group, Inc.:*Studying for a Driver's License*

No driver may wear radio earplugs. Drivers also many not wear headphones that cover both ears.

There may be a TV in a vehicle. Yet, no TV may be placed where the TV screen can be seen by the driver.

No one may drive a vehicle when things inside the vehicle limit the driver's view of the road to the front and side. Passengers also may not limit the driver's view of the road to the front and side.

Things packed in a vehicle may keep the driver from driving in a safe way. A car that is loaded with bags of groceries and boxes is an example of a packed vehicle. Passengers must not keep the driver from driving in a safe way.

No one may drive a vehicle with a child or other person seated between the driver and the steering wheel. Animals also many not be between the driver and the steering wheel.

CHECK YOUR STATE MANUAL Almost every state has laws to regulate vehicle restraints. Most states say that persons over 16 years of age must make sure their restraint is put on the right way. Yet, it is the driver's job to make sure persons under 16 have their restraint put on safely.

Drive Smart!

Directions: Read each sentence. If the sentence is true, put an X in the TRUE box. If the sentence if false, put an X in the FALSE box. Rewrite each false sentence making it true.

1. The state in which you live says that all front seat passengers must use safety restraints.

    ☐ TRUE   ☐ FALSE

    _____

    _____

    _____

2. The state in which you live says that all passengers in the back seat must use safety restraints.

    ☐ TRUE   ☐ FALSE

    _____

    _____

    _____

3. The state in which you live does not permit a driver to wear two headphones or use earplugs when driving.

☐ TRUE   ☐ FALSE

_____

_____

_____

4. The state in which you live has a law limiting the number of persons who can ride in the front seat.

☐ TRUE   ☐ FALSE

_____

_____

_____

5. The state in which you live has a law that says drivers may not carry an animal or passenger on their lap.

☐ TRUE   ☐ FALSE

_____

_____

_____

The People's Publishing Group, Inc.:*Studying for a Driver's License*

Hints to Help You Pass that Test!

Hints on Studying for Your Driver's Test

Now that you have finished reading this book, you will be asked to take one last test. The test is very much like the written driver's license tests in every state. Before taking this test, you should go back and study what you have learned.

Here are some hints on how to study for this test:

Hint # 1

Remember that you need to know all the traffic laws, signs, signals, and pavement markings in this book to be a safe driver. Last minute cramming is trying to remember everything just to pass the test. Yet, it will not work for a written driver's test. The facts you know today you will be using in days ahead! Take time to study everything well.

Hint # 2

Reread any parts of the book where some of the facts confuse you. Reread facts that you cannot remember.

Hint # 3

Have someone who drives ask you questions such as, "What does a white arrow curving to the right mean when it is painted on the pavement?"

Hint # 4

Make a set of flash card for signs, signals, and pavement markings. Go over them several times before taking the test.

Hint # 5

Reread all the tests you have already taken in this book. These tests covered much of what you need to know. Go back and correct any questions you got wrong.

Have a friend quiz you by asking old test questions. Check back in the book on any questions or words you cannot quickly and correctly answer.

Hint # 6

Have something healthy to eat before you take the test.

Hint # 7

Try to relax. Tests can be fun when you have taken the time to study and you know your facts!

Drive Smart Final Test

Directions: This is your final test. It is very much like the test you will take to get your driver's license. Think hard, before you answer each question.

1. A person who gets a license to driver a car can drive
   ___ a. a school bus.
   ___ b. trucks designed to haul more than 26,000 pounds.
   ___ c. a motorcycle.
   ___ d. a car, pickup or other private passenger vehicle.

2. When a person goes to take their driver's test and the vehicle they are driving is found to be unsafe, they
   ___ a. will be given a traffic ticket.
   ___ b. can get their license if they promise to get the vehicle fixed.
   ___ c. cannot take a road test in the vehicle.
   ___ d. will have to wait one year to get their license.

3. When a person without glasses tests less than 20/70, and a "corrective lenses" restriction is stamped on his or her license, this means they
   ___ a. can drive until they get their glasses and then be retested.
   ___ b. can drive during daylight hours without glasses.
   ___ c. can drive without glasses in an emergency.
   ___ d. must wear glasses whenever they drive.

4. It is unlawful to follow a fire engine, when it is being driven to a fire, at a distance of less than
   ___ a. 100 feet.   ___ b. 300 feet.
   ___ c. 500 feet.   ___ d. 700 feet.

5. It is legal to pass another vehicle on the right
   ___ a. anytime the vehicle ahead is driving less than the speed limit.
   ___ b. anytime there are two or more lanes of traffic moving in each direction.
   ___ c. anytime as long as you sound your horn.
   ___ d. under no conditions.

6. When passing another vehicle, drivers must return to the right lane
   ___ a. 100 feet before meeting an oncoming vehicle.
   ___ b. 150 feet before meeting an oncoming vehicle.
   ___ c. 200 feet before meeting an oncoming vehicle.
   ___ d. 250 feet before meeting an oncoming vehicle.

7. When a following driver wants to pass, the driver to be passed should
   ___ a. drive close to the center line and slow down.
   ___ b. increase speed to prevent the driver from passing.
   ___ c. drive in the center of the road until they are sure if is safe.
   ___ d. maintain a steady speed and move to the right side of their lane.

8. A driver on a two-lane road hears a siren, looks in the mirror, and sees a police car coming from behind with it's lights flashing. The driver should
   ___ a. steer to the right side of the road and stop.
   ___ b. stop as quickly as possible in the lane of travel.
   ___ c. increase speed to stay ahead of the police car.
   ___ d. keep going until it is possible to turn into a side road.

9. A signal for a turn from a highway must be given at least
   ___ a. 50 feet before the turn.
   ___ b. 100 feet before the turn.
   ___ c. 200 feet before the turn.
   ___ d. three or four seconds before the turn.

10. If a driver is involved in a crash, it must be reported to the police whether or not anyone is injured or if damage is
    ___ a. greater than $250.   ___ b. greater than $500.
    ___ c. greater than $1,000.   ___ d. any amount.

11. If a driver hits a parked vehicle and cannot find the owner or other driver, he or she must
    ___ a. leave their name and address fastened on the struck vehicle.
    ___ b. call a wrecker and have the other vehicle towed to a garage.
    ___ c. stay at the wreck until the other driver or owner comes back.
    ___ d. try to find the owner, if the owner cannot be found drive on.

12. When following another vehicle at night, drivers must dim their headlights at least
    ___ a. 200 feet behind the vehicle ahead.
    ___ b. 300 feet behind the vehicle ahead.
    ___ c. 350 feet behind the vehicle ahead.
    ___ d. 500 feet behind the vehicle ahead.

13. Under good traffic, weather, and road conditions, driving a vehicle fifteen (15) miles per hour slower than other traffic
    ___ a. is a good idea.
    ___ b. is always a safe way to drive.
    ___ c. is unlawful if it blocks other traffic.
    ___ d. is OK if your vehicle is old and unsafe.

14. Reckless driving is the act of
    ___ a. driving at a speed ten (10) mph over the speed limit.
    ___ b. committing two or more traffic violations at the same time.
    ___ c. driving with a complete lack of care or concern for the safety of others.
    ___ d. receiving a traffic violation for driving with a broken headlight.

15. A hand or signal light warning is required
    ___ a. whenever another driver is following too close.
    ___ b. whenever a driver is slowing, stopping, turning or changing lanes.
    ___ c. whenever a driver does not know what another driver wants to do.
    ___ d. when driving away from a stop sign or traffic signal.

16. The driver of a vehicle coming out of an alley, driveway or building must
    ___ a. slow and check traffic.
    ___ b. slow and blow the horn.
    ___ c. stop and give right of way to all road users.
    ___ d. stop and look both ways.

17. When a driver comes to a corner where a person with a white cane is waiting to cross the street, the driver must
    ___ a. slow to twenty (20) mph.
    ___ b. blow the horn to warn the pedestrian.
    ___ c. stop and grant right-of-way.
    ___ d. move to the second lane if there is one.

Drive Smart! Drive Safe! Drive Smart! Drive Safe! Drive Smart! Drive Safe! Drive Smart! Drive Safe! Drive Smart!

The People's Publishing Group, Inc.:*Studying for a Driver's License*

18. A driver is presumed to be driving while intoxicated, or DWI, if his or her blood alcohol concentration is
    ___ a. 0.00 - 0.04%.   ___ b. 0.05 - 0.07%.
    ___ c. 0.08% or greater.   ___ d. 0.10% or greater.

19. When stopped for an alcohol offense, a driver who refuses to take a test for Blood Alcohol Concentration may, under the "implied consent" law, have his or her driver's license suspended for
    ___ a. thirty (30) days.   ___ b. sixty (60) days.
    ___ c. ninety (90) days.   ___ d. up to a year.

20. A driver is parking a vehicle on a street near a railroad crossing. When parked, the vehicle must be at least
    ___ a. fifty (50) feet from the nearest rail.
    ___ b. one hundred (100) feet from the nearest rail.
    ___ c. twenty five (25) feet from the nearest rail;
    ___ d. seventy five (75) feet from the nearest rail.

21. A driver must park no less than ___ feet from a fire hydrant.
    ___ a. five (5) feet   ___ b. ten (10) feet
    ___ c. fifteen (15) feet   ___ d. twenty (20) feet

22. When driving in traffic with an escape path to one side, a driver should keep a following distance no less than
    ___ a. one car length per 10 miles per hour.
    ___ b. two seconds behind the vehicle ahead.
    ___ c. whatever the driver feel is safe.
    ___ d. three or four seconds behind the vehicle ahead.

23. If your car breaks down when driving on a highway at night, you should
    ___ a. raise the hood, turn off the headlights, and tie a white cloth to the left door handle.
    ___ b. park well off the road, turn off the headlights, and turn on the parking lights.
    ___ c. park well off the road, turn off the headlights, and turn on the emergency flashers;
    ___ d. park well off the road, turn on the bright lights, and parking lights.

24. When driving at night, you should not use high beam headlights when
    ___ a. slowing for a turn or exiting an expressway.
    ___ b. driving on a two lane road in the country.
    ___ c. driving down a long hill.
    ___ d. following with 200 feet of another vehicle.

25. The correct hand signal for a right turn is the driver's
    ___ a. left hand and arm extended out and up from the left side of the vehicle.
    ___ b. left hand and arm extended out and down from the left side of the vehicle.
    ___ c. left hand and arm extended straight out from the left side of the vehicle.
    ___ d. right hand and arm raised with the fingers pointing to the right.

Directions: You will now have twelve questions about signs. First, look at the picture. Next, read the four choices. Then, draw a line under the choice that correctly matches the sign.

1.
   a. Drivers in this lane must turn left.
   b. Drivers in this lane may go straight.
   c. Drivers in this lane must stop.
   d. Drivers in this lane have right-of-way.

2.
   a. Drivers can pass if it is safe to do so.
   b. Oncoming drivers may pass.
   c. Drivers can pass if the speed limit is less than 30.
   d. Drivers cannot cross these lines to pass.

3.
   a. Drivers must stop. They may go when it is safe to do so.
   b. Drivers must slow, and stop if something is coming.
   c. Drivers do not have to stop after dark.
   d. A pedestrian can wave you across the intersection.

4.
   a. All drivers must stop.
   b. Drivers who are turning left must stop
   c. Drivers must slow and be ready to stop.
   d. Drivers who are turning right must stop.

5.
   a. You must stop at the railroad crossing.
   b. There is a railroad crossing ahead.
   c. This railroad crossing is no longer used.
   d. One-way traffic at the railroad crossing.

6.
   a. Drivers moving in either direction use this lane to turn left.
   b. Drivers can use this lane to pass.
   c. Enter this lane a block before your turn.
   d. This lane cannot be used by trucks.

7.
   a. Drivers must stop for an oncoming train.
   b. If there is a train coming, it will stop.
   c. Caution railroad tracks ahead.
   d. Drivers must slow to 45 mph.

8.
   a. Maximum safe speed permitted if conditions are good.
   b. Maximum speeds only during daytime.
   c. Only cars can travel at this speed.
   d. It is always safe to drive at this speed.

9.
   a. Drivers may turn left. Traffic coming across the intersection has a red signal.
   b. Only traffic not making turns may move.
   c. Right turn on red is not permitted.
   d. Only traffic turning left may go. All others must stop.

10.
    a. Safe speed 45 mph.
    b. Any speed as long as you can make it.
    c. Safe speed 30 mph or less.
    d. Slow to 30 only if it is wet or icy.

11.
    a. School crossing zone one block ahead.
    b. Be alert for children. There is a school within one block of street.
    c. Ignore the sign if it is Saturday or Sunday, there is no school.
    d. There will always be a crossing guard if children are around.

12.
    a. Pedestrians should not cross the street.
    b. Pedestrians can cross if they hurry.
    c. If pedestrians are not half way across the street, they should turn back.
    d. All traffic will soon stop so that pedestrians can cross.

Drive Smart! Drive Safe! Drive Smart! Drive Safe! Drive Smart! Drive Safe! Drive Smart! Drive Safe! Drive Smart!

WORDS TO KNOW

TERM	ENGLISH DEFINITION	SPANISH DEFINITION
Airbag	A special bag that blows up to protect a person during a crash.	Una bolsa especial que se infla para proteger a una persona durante una colisión.
Average speed	The speed at which most vehicles are moving.	La velocidad promedio de los vehículos en movimiento.
Billboard	A large sign with a message about the road or traffic.	Un mensaje acerca del tráfico o la carretera escrito en un cartel muy grande.
Brake	That part of the vehicle that lets the driver bring the vehicle to a stop.	Parte del vehículo que permite al conductor detener el vehículo.
Brake light	A red light on the back of a vehicle that lights up when the driver steps on the brake pedal.	Una luz roja en la parte trasera del vehículo que se enciende cuando el conductor presiona el pedal de freno.
Center line	The line that divides traffic going in different or opposite ways.	La línea que divide el tráfico que circula en direcciónes diferentes u opuestas.
Construction	A place where road work is taking place.	Area en la cual se está construyendo o reparando carreteras.
Construction zone	A place where road work is taking place.	Un lugar donde se está haciendo trabajo en las carreteras.
Crash	One vehicle hitting another vehicle or object.	Un vehículo que choca con otro vehículo u objecto.
Cross	To go from one side of the road to another.	Ir de un lado de la calle al lado opuesto.
Curve	A bend in the road.	Un doblaje en la carretera.
Detour	To leave the road you want to drive on because the road you want to use is closed.	Tomar otra carretera porque la que desea está cerrada.
Driving to the right	To drive to the right side of the street.	Conducir del lado derecho de la calle.
Emergency vehicle	A vehicle with flashing lights and a siren used to respond to calls for help.	Un vehículo con luces intermitentes y sirena usado para responder a llamados de ayuda urgente.
Exit	Leave an area.	Abandonar el area.
FT.	Feet (12 inches equals 1 foot).	Pie (12 pulgadas equivale a 1 pie.)
Funeral procession	A number of vehicles driving in line to honor someone who has died.	Un número de vehículos que se mueven juntos en fila con el propósito de honrar a alguien que ha muerto.
Guide	To show you the way.	Mostrar el camino.
Headlight	One of two or four lights on the front of a vehicle.	Una de dos o cuatro luces localizadas en el frente de un vehículo.
High speed roadway	A highway, freeway or other road with limited access.	Una carretera, autopista u otra vía con acceso limitado.
Highway	A road used by vehicles. Other words used for highway are road, street, and roadway.	Una carretera usada por vehículos. Otras palabras usadas son calle, autopista y vía.
ID	Short for identification.	Abreviatura de identificación.
Insurance	A written contract that keeps you from having to pay a large amount of money in case of a crash.	Un contrato por escrito que evita que tenga que pagar mucho dinero en caso de una colisión.
Interchange entrance	A special one-way road that takes vehicles off a high speed roadway.	Carretera especial de una sola vía a los vehículos hacia una autopista de alta velocidad.
Interchange	Takes the place of an intersection and lets vehicles move from one road to another by changing speed and place to move smoothly into traffic without stopping.	Toma la función de una intersección al dejar que los vehículos e muevan de una carretera a otra y con solo cambiar la velocidad puedan entrar en el tráfico sin detenerse.
Interchange exit	A special one-way road that takes vehicles onto a high-speed roadway.	Carretera especial de una sola vía que lleva a los vehículos hacia una autopista de alta velocidad.
Intersection	Where two roads join, connect, or cross.	Donde dos carreteras se unen, conectano se cruzan.

WORDS TO KNOW

TERM	ENGLISH DEFINITION	SPANISH DEFINITION
Interstate	A road that often crosses over two or more states.	Una carretera que cruza dos o mas estados.
Junction	Where two roads meet.	Donde dos carreteras se unen.
Lane	An area divided by white or yellow lines.	Un área dividida por líneas blancas o amarillas.
Legal	To agree with the law.	De acuercdo con la ley.
Lens	The covering of a signal light.	Parte que cubre el bombillo de un semáforo.
License	A card that shows that a person has passed all state tests needed to drive.	Un documento que muestra que una persona ha pasado todos los exámenes requeridos por el estado para conducir.
Lien	A statement of ownership of a vehicle by the person or business you are borrowing money from to buy a vehicle.	Declaración de propiedad de un vehículo por la persona o negocio la cual le ha prestado dinero para comprarlo.
Limited access	Drivers can get on or off the road only at an interchange.	Los conductores pueden entrar en o salir de la cerretera solo a traves de una vía altena.
Maximum speed	The fastest speed you are allowed to travel.	La velocidad mas alta a la cual la ley le permite conducir.
Median	A center paved area that runs between lanes of traffic traveling in opposite directions.	Area central pavimentada situada entre vías de tráfico que se mueven en direcciones opuestas.
Message sign	Uses lights to tell drivers about road conditions.	Usa luces para advertir a los conductores acerca de las condiciones del tráfico.
Minimum speed	The slowest speed you are allowed to travel.	La velocidad mas lenta a la cual la ley le permite conducir.
MPH	The number of miles traveled in one hour.	El número de millas recorridas en una hora.
Oncoming traffic	Traffic coming toward you.	El tráfico que viene hacia usted.
Parallel	To park in line with something, such as a curb, or road edge.	Estacionarse en línea con la acera o el borde de la carretera.
Parking brake (emergency brake)	That part of the brake system that holds a vehicle in place after it has been stopped.	Parte del sistema de freno que mantiene el vehículo en su lugar despues de haberlo detenido.
Parking lights	Two small orange lights on the front of a vehicle and two red of the back on the back of a vehicle.	Dos pequeñas luces color naranja localizadas al frente del vehículo y dos luces rojas en la parte trasera del vehiculo.
Pass	To catch up and get ahead, or in front of, another vehicle.	Alcanzar y adelantarse o avanzar al frente de otro vehículo.
Passenger	Anyone who rides in a vehicle.	Cualquier persona que va sentada en un vehículo.
Pavement	The hard surface of a road.	La superficie dura de una carretera.
Pedestrian	Any person walking on or across a roadway.	Una persona que camina o cruza una calle.
Permit	A card that lets a person drive for a short time while the person prepares to take the driver's test.	Un documento que autoriza a una persona conducir por cierto tiempo mientras que está se prepara para tomar el examen de conducción.
Recreation	Something people do to relax and enjoy themselves.	Actividad que se hace para entrenerse o descansar.
Register	To get license plates for a vehicle so you can drive it on the road.	Obtener un número de placas para un vehiculo, y asi, poder manejarlo en la calle.
Regulate	To tell what can and cannot be done.	Decir lo que se puede o no se puede hacer.
Regulatory	Saying what can and cannot be done.	Accion de decir lo que se puede o no se puede hacer.
Reversible	Being able to be used in an opposite way.	Lo que puede ser usado de forma contraria.
Revoke	To take away someone's license.	Quitarle a alguien su licencia de conducir.
Right-of-Way	One driver is given the right to move before another driver moves.	Cuando a un conductor se le permite mover su vehículo antes que a cualquier otro conductor.

WORDS TO KNOW

TERM	ENGLISH DEFINITION	SPANISH DEFINITION
Risk	To take a chance.	Tomar un riesgo.
Route	A road that can be traveled on.	Una calle que se puede transitar.
Safety restraint	A belt that holds a person on the seat of the vehicle.	El cinturón que sujeta a una persona al asiento del vehículo.
School zone	An area around a school.	Area a los alrededores de una de una escuela.
Shared	A lane being used by more than one vehicle.	Una línea que es usada por mas de un vehículo.
Signal	To tell other road users where you are or what you want to do.	Decirle a los otros conductores donde usted está o lo que desea hacer.
Signal lamp	A brake light, turn signal, or emergency flasher.	Una luz de freno, luz direccional o luz de emergencia.
Speed limit	The speed you may by law travel on the street.	La velocidad a la cual la ley le permite conducir.
Stand a vehicle	When the driver stays in the vehicle while it is stopped for a short time.	Cuando el conductor se queda en el vehículo cuando está estacionado por corto tiempo.
Steer	To guide a vehicle by holding the steering wheel and turning it right or left.	Guiar un vehículo sujetando el timón y volteandolo hacia la derecha o hacia la izquierda.
Suspend	To take away a right for a length of time.	Quitarle a alguien un derecho por cierto tiempo.
Suspension	Taking away of a driver's license for a certain amount of time. This could be 30, 60, 90, or 180 days.	Quitarle a un chofer su licencia de conducir por cierto tiempo. Puede ser por 30, 60, 90, o 180 días.
Title	A paper given by the state that shows who owns a vehicle.	Un documento dado por el estado que indica quien es el dueño de un vehículo.
Traffic law	A rule that tells you what to do, or not to do, when driving.	Una regulación que le indica lo que debe, o no debe hacer cuando conduce.
Traffic island	A solid area that divides traffic.	Un área sólida que divide el tráfico.
Traffic control device	Something used to guide, warn, or direct drivers.	Instrumento usado para guiar, advertir, o dirigir a los conductores.
Traffic signal	A sign or light that warns or directs drivers to take some action.	Una señal o luz que advierte o indica acciones a tomar a los condutores.
Traffic sign	A sign that tells drivers what they need to know.	Una señal que le dice a los conductores lo que necesitan saber.
Traffic offense	Doing something against a traffic law.	Hacer algo en contra de las leyes del tráfico.
Tread	That part of the tire that touches the road.	La parte de la rueda que está en contacto con la carretera.
Turn	A move to another street at or into a driveway or parking space.	Voltear en una esquina y entrar en otra calle, entrar en una entrada privada o estacionamiento.
Two-lane road	A road with two lanes of traffic, one lane of traffic moving in one direction and the other lane of traffic moving in the opposite direction.	Una carretera de dos vias en la que el tráfico de una vía se mueve en una direccion, mientras que el tráfico en la otra vía se mueve en direccion opuesta.
Vehicle	Any car, truck, bus, bicycle, or anything else with wheels that can by law use a road.	Un auto, camión, bus, bicicleta o método e transporte rodante autorizado para usar las carreteras.
Warning devices	Horns and sirens used to alert drivers and other road users.	Bocinas y sirenas usadas para alertar a los conductores y otros usuarios.
Windshield	The large area of glass on the front of a vehicle.	Area grande de cristal en el frente del vehículo.
Zone	A special area.	Un área específica.

The People's Publishing Group, Inc.:*Studying for a Driver's License*